EARLY COUNTRY MOTORING

CARS AND MOTORCYCLES IN SUFFOLK 1896–1940

My father, Fruer Bridges, with his 1932 Morris Major.

EARLY COUNTRY MOTORING

CARS AND MOTORCYCLES IN SUFFOLK 1896–1940

JOHN F. BRIDGES

Published by John F. Bridges, Little Waldingfield, Suffolk

Printed and bound in Great Britain by
The Wolsey Press, Ipswich, Suffolk

British Library Cataloguing-in-Publication Data
A catalogue record for this book is available from the British Library

ISBN 0 9505148 1 0

*This book is dedicated to the memory of
Robert Fulker and John Western*

CONTENTS

ACKNOWLEDGEMENTS

In researching this book, I have been helped by many people who willingly gave me access to their memories, photographs and records. It has been a most enjoyable experience and I would like to record my thanks to them all.

Morgan Watts provided the initial spark for this project, with his recollections of Framlingham in the period before the First World War and his vivid memories of early motoring. Sadly, Morgan, and several of those mentioned below, died before this book was published.

John Mumford provided much useful information on Botwoods, based on his earlier research. Enoch Akester joined Botwood & Egerton in 1908, and it was an unexpected privilege for me to find someone who, at the age of 100, could recall those times from personal experience. Nic Portway, as well as giving me much general assistance, provided many interesting sources of information that never ceased to surprise me. Michael Ashwell and John Potter gave free access to the A.G. Potter archives, which contain a wealth of detail that so rarely survives nowadays.

The photographic identification of early cars is a specialist task, and I am indebted to David Hales for his assistance in this matter. Also, thanks to Geoff Clarke for reproducing several of the photographs. I am grateful to Peter Brockes of the National Motor Museum, Beaulieu for checking the text.

I should like to thank all the individuals who assisted me: Mr Adams, Miss L. Ambrose, W.G. Arnott, Michael Atkinson, Walter Bailey, Jack Barnard, Ernest Birkett, G. Blewitt, Kenneth Bond, Jeremy Brett, Victor Brewster, Percy Bridges, John Brunskill, Sir George Burton, Tony Cardy, Glory Chenery, Albert Child, Laurence Coe, John Collinson, Lance Cooper, Peter Corder, Noel Cotton, Aubrey Deeks, Harley Deschamps, John Digby, Harry Double, W. Dowsing, Percy Eastaugh, Bill Ellis, Michael Elmer, Don French, Ronald Gosling, Peter Hansford, A. Haste, Diana Howard, O.J. Jarman, L. Kerridge, Dave Kindred, Clifford Last, John Lacy Scott, J. Mallett, Bob Malster, Tony Martin, Miss M.I. Metcalfe, Charles Minter, John Moore, Sidney Moore, Derrick Neave, John Olorenshaw, Brigadier J.J. Packard, Mr Paskall, Frank Pearl, W. Pike, Ann Pilgrim, Bob Plant, J. Postans, Geoff Revett, Gordon Robinson, D. Sarginson, Ron Sayer, Basil Smith, David Steed, Bob Stirling, Stephen Sullivan, Colin Turner, Leonard Wardley, A. West, R. Wright – and my apologies to any others I may have inadvertently forgotten.

The following organisations gave me valuable assistance and information: the *Bury Free Press*, Theo Cutting; *Classic Motor Cycle*, Kim White and Brian Wooley; *East Anglian Daily Times*; East Anglian Film Archive, David Cleveland; Ford of Europe Incorporated, David Burgess Wise; Ipswich Transport Museum, Mike Abbott and Chris Haste; Mann Egerton & Co Ltd, Marie Lee and Florence Wright; The National Motor Museum, Beaulieu, Annice Collett; The Photographic Workshop, David Spall; Punch Publications Ltd, Miranda Taylor; Suffolk Constabulary, Superintendent Jolley and PC Evans; Suffolk Record Office, all staff at Ipswich, Bury St Edmunds and Lowestoft; University of Reading, Dr J.H. Brown; The Vintage Motor Cycle Club Ltd, W. E. Hume.

Special thanks to Anita Spall, Sheila Blyth and Joan Clark of Acoustic Design Ltd for their word-processing skills; and to my patient family, Pat, Susannah and Robert, who put up with my countless visits to all parts of the county and long periods of confinement in the study.

The frustrations of trying to have this book published finally led me to have a go myself. A big thank-you, therefore, to my sister Ann, whose editing and desktop publishing expertise has made it all possible.

The cover to this book was to have been an early motoring scene painted by my friend John Western. He had always been very interested in cars and motorcycles, and was excited at the prospect of combining a motoring scene with a well-known Suffolk view. His tragic death in 1993 ended a rare talent, and he is greatly missed.

Photographs and illustrations on the following pages kindly provided by:
E. Birkett, 6, 56, 57, 58, 67, 68, 70; G. Blewitt, 119; J. Brett, 107, back cover; V . Brewster, 43; J. Brooke, 101, 106; G. Burton, 137; G. Chenery, 128; J. Collinson, 142, 143, 144; L. Coe, 42; L. Cooper, 14, 41; P. Corder, 146 (1); Cowie's, 20; A. Deeks, 49, 75, 76; H. Deschamps, 149; *East Anglian Daily Times*, 115; D. French, 134; R. Gosling, 120; D. Hales, 114, 117 ; P. Hansford, 32, 100, 103, 105; O. Jarman, 4, 29; J. Kerridge, 21; D. Kindred (via D. Cotton), 38, 52, 140, 141; C. Last, 129; H. Lord, 146 (2); J. Mallett, 66; R. Markham, 145; Mann Egerton & Co Ltd, 11, 72, 73, 74; D. Neave, 138; F. Pearl, 45, 46, 47; N. Portway, front cover, 2, 16, 25, 36, 50, 59, 63, 65, 104; A.G. Potter, 19, 78, 81, 85, 87, 88, 89, 91, 93, 96; Punch Publications Ltd, 9; Mr Pye, 51; G. Revett, 139; G. Robinson, 44 ; H. Ruse, 7; L. Sewell, 54; B. Smith, 147, 148; Chief Constable, Suffolk Constabulary, 110; Suffolk Record Office, 3, 5, 24, 35, 93, 113, 116, 125, 136; J. Watts, 130; R. Wright, 34.
Other material is from the author's collection.

FOREWORD

I am proud to have been born in Suffolk, and to have the opportunity of providing a link to the Brooke cars that were manufactured in the county at the beginning of this century. The family albums and scrapbooks have, I believe, contributed in some small way to this remarkable and wide-ranging book, which embraces so much detail that might otherwise be lost in a few years' time.

We are indebted to John Bridges for the research and painstaking effort he has taken over the last ten years. The list of acknowledgements bears testimony to that, and the final result provides a fascinating view of the changes brought about in the county from the turn of the century to the Second World War.

My grandfather Mawdsley started driving in 1898, and went on to develop the first three-cylinder Brooke in 1901. The twelve years during which Brooke built cars were but a short period in the history of the company – which existed from 1875 to 1993 – but must have been the most exciting time, with the rapid development of the internal combustion engine and all that led from it.

John has compiled a book that brings to life all the enthusiasm and energy with which Suffolk people took on the impact of the horseless carriage in all its many aspects. The problems encountered by those early motorists are difficult to appreciate as we approach the centenary of the car, and this book provides an absorbing insight into those pioneering days.

J.D.M. Brooke, 1995

INTRODUCTION

For many people who live in the country, the motor car is an integral part of everyday life, essential to reach their place of work, transport the week's shopping, or visit the seaside at the weekend. However, this is a comparatively recent phenomenon, and even after the Second World War most people would not have believed that so many families today would have at least one car.

At the turn of the century even the sight of a motor car would have caused major excitement. These early cars were usually owned by the adventurous wealthy classes, who now required a chauffeur, and possibly a mechanic, as well as a coachman.

The motor car was certainly a novelty, with its noisy internal combustion engine announcing its arrival. The people who decided that there was possibly some future in these machines were often cycle dealers, as they had a natural affinity with anything mechanical. The firms that hired horses and carriages did not usually respond well to the car, and saw it as a short-lived threat to their long-established trade. After a few years, however, their advertisements would indicate that a car was also available for hire, and eventually the coach side disappeared altogether. The major coach manufacturers usually saw the writing on the wall from an early age, and seized the opportunity to make the bodies for the new horseless carriages.

Many established firms in other lines of business bought a car for private hire work and then developed a motor business from it. Blacksmiths, although involved with the repair of broken parts, did not generally make the transition into the motor trade.

The road conditions for the motorist at the turn of this century were very poor. In the 1830s the roads had improved considerably due to the tolls charged, and it was the golden age of coach travel. One of the last great coaching inns to be built in the country was the Bell at Saxmundham, in 1842. By this time, though, coach travel was in serious decline, and by the middle of the 19th century the railways had opened up their vast network. This took much of the traffic from the roads and canals, with the effect that the road conditions deteriorated badly as there was less money for maintenance. No wonder the early motorists were pioneers; they had to be prepared for all manner of mishaps to themselves and their motor cars.

The aim of this book is to give an insight into the development of private motoring in Suffolk up to around 1940, concentrating more on the people and places rather than the technicalities of the vehicles. Most of the original businesses have now disappeared, along with any record of their existence. The two companies that are considered in some detail here – Botwoods of Ipswich, and Potters of Framlingham – have been chosen as they represent opposite ends of the spectrum. The former developed from a large established coach-building firm which had contacts with well-known motoring pioneers. J.R. Egerton was a partner in the company during the first decade of the century, and probably did more to promote motoring in Suffolk than anyone else. Although I never met him, many people called him Reggie and I have done so in this book. He did not use his first name Justin, and Reginald sounds too formal for such a dynamic character. Botwoods was eventually taken over by Mann Egerton & Co Ltd, but the Botwoods name was retained until the early 1970s, when several Mann Egerton companies were merged under one name.

Potters of Framlingham is perhaps more typical, evolving from a small cycle business which grew slowly and eventually obtained the Ford agency – which it still holds to this day.

There has been no attempt to cover all the early motor businesses in the county, due to both lack of data and space. The book has been written in a form which I hope will be of interest to Suffolk people and motoring enthusiasts alike. For this reason the two chapters on particular companies are not complete histories, but are intended to portray the general atmosphere of those formative years.

The early days of A.G. Potter are partly based on the memories of Morgan Watts, who was the first employee. I had known him for several years and was aware of his bicycle business, but it was not until I interviewed him at length that the detail of those early years came into focus and made me realise how much we take for granted in our everyday motoring. I have included his exploits in the First World War as they are an integral part of his early life and very much related to motoring.

An attempt has been made to record the manufacturers of cars in Suffolk, although research in this area is never ending. Technical descriptions are included for some of the cars in order to record the achievements of these pioneers.

Motorcycling is a particular interest of mine, and the final chapter looks at the early development of two-wheeled transport. Commercial vehicles are included only where they form an important link with the main theme.

John F. Bridges, 1995
Little Waldingfield, Suffolk

CHAPTER ONE

THE HORSELESS CARRIAGE
1896–1918

T he daily needs of transport and heavy toil in the country had for centuries been performed by the horse, and in our county the might of the Suffolk Punch is legendary. However, towards the end of the last century, developments were taking place on the continent with an alternative source of power: the internal combustion engine. This found a natural place in the existing coaches of the day, resulting in the new 'horseless carriage'. Slowly, the pattern of life established around the horse was to change, but there was much opposition to it.

In this country, development of the motor car was severely hindered in the latter part of the 19th century by restrictive legislation. The 'Red Flag' Act of 1865 stated that any machine-powered device must have a minimum of three drivers, a maximum speed of 2mph in town, 4mph in the country, and a footman 60 yards in front with a red flag. Although the red flag became optional in 1878, a man was still required to walk 20 yards in front. This legislation was aimed at the very heavy steam-powered traction engines using the roads at that time. And there was some justification for this: they could do considerable damage, as witnessed by accounts of one knocking down the wall of a house in Eastgate Street, Bury St Edmunds, when its steering chain broke.

Meanwhile, England pressed on with its perfection of the bicycle, which was produced on a small scale in town and village workshops, and mass-produced in cities such as Coventry. It seems difficult to believe today, but at the end of the 19th century there was considerable hostility towards cycling, and many people thought it should not be allowed on Sundays. Others suggested that cyclists should pay taxes and that this money be used on the roads. A comment in the *Bury Free Press* of 1897 stated, 'The recklessness displayed by some riders is very gross, and it would be a wise step if the Borough Authorities were to put a stop to "scorching" in the town and immediate neighbourhood.' Against this background, the fledgling motorist was an obvious target for complaints.

The first cars were imported into this country around 1895, and used on private roads. They were invariably from France or Germany, as these two countries were not hampered by restrictive legislation. Pioneering names included Benz, Daimler, Panhard et Levassor, Peugeot, and De Dion Bouton, some of which are still familiar to us today.

Combs tannery, c. 1900. Joseph Webb, with bowler hat, is seated on a Benz Viktoria of c. 1896–8. Powered by a rear-mounted 5hp engine, the term 'horseless carriage' is most appropriate.

It was not until 1896 that the 'Red Flag Act' (Locomotives Act, 1865) was amended to allow a speed increase to 14mph, although it was subsequently reduced to 12mph by the Local Government Board. This new freedom was celebrated by the first London to Brighton Run, with some thirty solid-tyred cars competing.

On the day of emancipation, the following advertisement for insurance appeared in the *East Anglian Daily Times*:

> November 14th 1896, the day when motor carriages may use highways at a maximum speed of 12mph – an added peril to life and limb. Fellow townsmen, hurry up to 32 Westgate Street and relieve your trembling wives and poor children of these new risks.

Two days later, Ipswich witnessed its first motorised vehicle when Charles Berners of Woolverstone Park drove his De Dion powered tricycle into town to visit Mr Popplewell's cycle shop in the Woodbridge Road. Mr Berners had bought his machine in Paris several months earlier, but had only been able to use it in his private grounds until the new Act was introduced.

The *Bury Free Press* published an article on the London to Brighton run, and concluded with the following far-sighted comments:

> The Brightonian quadrupeds are said to have greeted that draggle tailed remnant [the cars that reached Brighton] with a neigh of scorn, but all the same, we

William Pretty and family in their Gobron Brillié, c. 1900. His wife Mable was also a keen motorist and the first woman to obtain an Ipswich driving licence, in 1904.

should be wrong to pronounce the motor car as a failure, or for a moment suppose it has not come to stay. It is in its callowest infancy at present, but it is destined to become a huge and mighty giant ere long, and it will work stupendous revolutions in the economy of daily life.

One can imagine the excitement caused in villages and towns by the appearance of the first motor car. As it was to be another seven years before registration became a legal requirement, the first cars in the county cannot be determined from such records as do exist. From various press cuttings it would appear that the first car to be seen in Bury St Edmunds, in 1896, was a solid-tyred Benz belonging to the Thetford firm of Charles Burrell & Sons, the well-known traction engine builders. How ironic that they should own the first vehicle of a type which would eventually kill off the product for which they had become established. Other early motorists in Bury were Dr Lucas of Angel Hill in 1899, and Mr Sparke, a solicitor, who owned a 1900 Lanchester with tiller steering. Also, Mr Reeman the vet, of Risbygate Street, had a single-cylinder De Dion Bouton. It was often the case that doctors, vets and auctioneers were the first to see the advantages of the new form of transport. When Henry Lacy Scott became lame from a bad horse accident, he vowed that if an alternative means of transport were to become available, he would make good use of it. Although he later acquired a driving licence, it seems he never did drive and was content to be chauffeured by his sons.

The Elveden Hall estate, c. 1903. Lord Iveagh is at the wheel of the Panhard, next to him is the Duke of York, later to become King George V. The second car is a 12hp four-cylinder Panhard, c. 1901, and was used when the royal party arrived at Thetford Station, either for luggage or a replacement in case of breakdown. The Duke enjoyed these shooting parties, which would last all week. On one such visit in 1899 he killed 368 pheasants, 177 partridges, 28 hares, 51 rabbits and a pig, using 1,200 cartridges.

A.F. Garnham, a well-known Ipswich motor agent, declared in 1901:

> Doctors in this town are rather behind the times in adopting motor cars for their work, but I am glad to say I have at last succeeded in making a start. Dr Moseley, of this town, is now using a very smart Benz Victoria with a hood and, after three weeks use, declares himself to be highly pleased with the satisfactory way in which the car does work.

There seems to have been a two- or three-year period after 'Emancipation' (Locomotives on Highways Act, 1896) before some of the well-off and adventurous people decided to try the new form of transport. It was not until June 1898 that the people of Suffolk saw a number of cars on the road, when the Automobile Club of Great Britain and Ireland (the ACGBI, later to become the RAC) organised a six-day tour of East Anglia. The arrival of the fourteen cars in Bury St Edmunds was watched with considerable interest by a large crowd of people. They then moved on to Norwich, where the party split in two before taking different routes to Ipswich. In most cases they were passing through towns and villages where the motor car had never been seen before. They met up again for luncheon at the Bell Hotel in Saxmundham, with Mr Ernest Quinton of Needham Market being one of the first to arrive, on a De Dion tricycle. The main vehicles appear to have been manufactured by either the Daimler Co or Benz, with one Bollée, described as 'very noisy but very fast'. Mr J.R. Jefferies of Ransomes, Sims & Jefferies came to examine the cars with a critical eye!

The *EADT* reporter was given a lift for the final journey to Ipswich, which he described as follows:

> This particular car was one of the first two ever built, it had travelled over 5,000 miles without a breakdown, and with no further repair than putting on new tyres, and was altogether, truth to tell, the oldest and shabbiest of the whole show. Going uphill was slow work, the engine pulling and gasping away in asthmatical

fashion. Along level stretches of road the motion was rapid yet so pleasant that there was apparently no element of excitement in the business, but going downhill was another thing altogether, and was very much like a prolonged run on the switchback railway. The driver explained that he could pull up within 10 yards no matter how hard he was going, though the sudden stoppage might throw the box seat passenger over the front of the car!

The car went a glorious pace into Woodbridge, and then a strange thing happened. At Woodbridge of all places in the world, the town that lived by the horse and almost worships the horse, the motor broke down and had to be dragged into the Bull Hotel yard, while horsey spectators offered sarcastic comments, asking whether the driver was going to give it a 'bran mash' and so forth. To make the irony of fate complete, it must for repair be sent to Coventry! There was many a laugh in Woodbridge over the incident on Monday night, no doubt, but for all that the motor car has come to stay.

The stranded reporter managed to get a lift in one of the other cars for the final run to Ipswich, where a reception was held at the Great White Horse Hotel. The reference to Coventry would indicate that the broken-down car was a Daimler.

By the turn of the century, the local authorities sensed that the motor car was not merely a passing novelty, and became concerned over its impact on the community and its highways. To redress the balance, the ACGBI invited the members of the Roads and Bridges Committee of the East Suffolk County Council to acquire a personal and practical knowledge of the control that drivers have over their vehicles. In 1901 they brought a number of cars to Lowestoft, Beccles and Ipswich for this purpose. The Committee was suitably 'enlightened' and felt that it would not be necessary to adopt a reduced speed limit of 10mph – a good public relations exercise.

At the same time, however, the Committee was also recommending that all cars should be numbered and registered, but there was considerable protest from certain

Charles and Emma Cotton of Grundisburgh on their Benz dogcart of c. 1900. As it bears an early East Suffolk registration, the photo must have been taken after 1903.

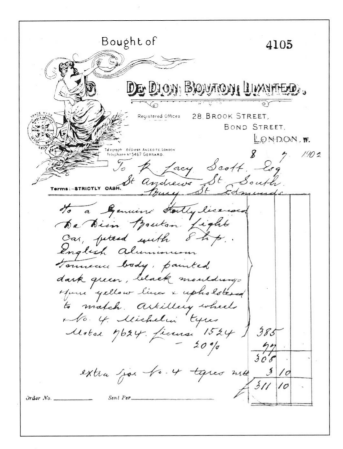

The 1904 Ipswich registrations show that 34 per cent of the cars were manufactured by De Dion Bouton. This 8hp model was purchased by Reginald Lacy Scott in 1902. It must have provided good service as he bought a newer model in 1910.

members. Motorists were not keen to be so easily labelled and identified. Reggie Egerton wrote to *The Autocar* in 1902 regarding an incident in which it was claimed that a horse had been startled by his car, and he had stopped to discuss the matter with its owner. *The Autocar* replied: 'It shows at once what sort of annoyance [registration] numbers would provide, as if his car had been numbered, he would have been identified in any case, whether he had stayed in the district or not, and although blameless, put to the annoyance and expense of defending an unjustifiable charge.' Despite many such protestations, all vehicles had to be registered from January 1904.

Ernest Ambrose recalled the impact of the early motor cars in his book *Melford Memories*:

> The villagers looked on the cars with very mixed feelings. I heard that in one Suffolk village the people piled farm wagons on the road to stop them, but Melford took them more philosophically, though nevertheless with much suspicion. The older men particularly disliked them and talk in the pubs was no longer about the rotation of the crops and kindred subjects, but these ' 'ere new fangled morty cars'. ''Tis the invention of the devil.' 'It 'ont last; it can't last; scares the 'osses out of their wits.' Some thought they were a mechanical toy to amuse the rich, and would die out in time. Many thought they were a public nuisance and motorists in general were dangerous lunatics.

These curious-looking inventions would often be drawn up outside a pub, and as some proud owner tinkered with his new model trying to start it up, such remarks as the following would be heard.

'Ain't she bufull?'

'Don't think nawthen to it mesen.'

'Must a corst a tidy bit.'

'That 'ere sheen 'ont stut.'

And from the tone of his voice, he sincerely hoped his words would be proved correct.

As the smart carriages and broughams of the wealthy were gradually ousted by motor cars, coachmen, grooms and stable boys had to learn (often very reluctantly) to struggle with clutches and gears. Some of the older men, who had lived with horses all their lives, couldn't get out of the habit of shouting 'Whoa'. Many were the noisy and hostile encounters on the roads. The horses were very frightened at the noisy contraptions which they met, and there were quite a lot of accidents, and as for the verbal encounters on the road, these were often highly inflammable, even to the point of blows.

One of the first cars in Melford was built by Mr Medcalf. An occasion arose when I had to go to Cambridge on urgent business. Mr Sewell, our manager, was very seriously ill and the only chance to save his life was for a specialist to operate on him without delay. There was no available telephone so Mr Medcalf agreed to take me there. The journey took over four hours and the engine broke down three times. Going through Horseheath we met some horses from Newmarket with their trainer and a stable boy. The horses took fright at our noisy machine and unseated the boy. Fortunately he hung on to the horse or it would have bolted. I managed to get to Cambridge in time to see the specialist and arrange with him to come over immediately to operate on Mr Sewell. But he dare

Medcalf's shop in Hall Street, Long Melford, was typical of most country businesses, repairing cars, motorcycles and bicycles. AR20 is a 5hp Humberette, first registered in Hertford in December 1903.

not risk coming back with us by car, instead he caught the last train back to Melford and was just in time to save Mr Sewell's life. We had to stop in Cambridge for the night as we daren't try to go back at night. The next day we made the return journey without serious mishap, though we had to stop several times to make adjustments to the machinery. If Mr Medcalf hadn't been such a skilled mechanic we should never have arrived at all.

Fred Sewell was a clever mechanic and never minded how long he spent on a job. One evening he was called out on some job just as he was about to close his shop in Hall Street, and he forgot to return. The next morning when he went to work, the shop door was still open, the light on, and his day's takings of little piles of coins on the counter as he had left it the night before. Fred had one of the earliest cars and enjoyed telling of his exploits with it. He and some friends planned a day's outing to Clacton. All went well for a few miles until from the back seat came shouts 'Whoa, Fred.' 'What's up?' 'Car's afire.' Smoke was seeping through the floor board and they found the straw padding of the back seat was alight. They soon remedied that, and on they went. The engine stalled once or twice and at the mere suggestion of a hill they all got out and pushed. Just within sight of Clacton another shout came from the back seat, 'Whoa, Fred.' 'What's up?' 'Car's afire agin.' Out they all climbed and dealt with that. Coming home the acetylene lights functioned only occasionally, but as they were travelling mostly through country lanes they didn't worry too much until they suddenly realised they had lost their way. 'Never mind,' said Fred, 'we'll keep gooing. We'll get somewhere. The moon'ull be up soon. That'ull show us the direction.' Suddenly there was another diversion. Going through a village they saw in the light of an open door of a pub, two men in full evening dress and top hats. They staggered outside and started fighting, encouraged by cheering onlookers. 'We marn't miss this.' So they stopped the car and enjoyed the spectacle. In due course they got near home and strange to relate just as they reached the top of Ballingdon Hill their flickering lamp came on again and stayed alight sufficiently for them to reach home in safety. All agreed it was a 'werry nice day's outing'.

The new horseless carriage was a strange curiosity and attracted considerable attention, much of it adverse. If some people resented bicycles, their attitude towards motor cars can hardly be imagined. As well as the problems of dust, noise, speed and the deterioration of the roads, there was also the threat to the established ways of life based around horse transport. Magistrates were often prejudiced against early motorists, irrespective of their rank or place in society. In 1903 a summons was served on Major Carthew of Woodbridge Abbey, alleging that he, 'being the driver of a certain carriage or light locomotive . . . did unlawfully drive the same at a greater speed than twelve miles an hour'. At Onehouse, near Stowmarket, in the same year, a man was charged with 'driving so furiously as to endanger the lives and limbs of passengers on the highway'. The defendant was said to have come round a corner suddenly without warning, causing a cob to shy and turn rapidly in the shafts of the phaeton, which were pressed against the wheel of the car. The 'furious' speed was gauged at 16mph, and the Bench imposed a fine of £1.

Apart from the prejudice, there was genuine concern that motor cars were a threat to pedestrians. On 14 November 1905, exactly nine years after the Emancipation Act, seven-year-old Allan Staines was knocked down by a car in Wherstead Road, Ipswich, and died almost instantly. He had been running along behind a carrier's cart and for some reason had darted out in front of the car, which had no chance of stopping. The coroner said that it was the first death caused by a motor car that he had investigated.

The general animosity shown towards motorists and the continual persecution by the police for speed-related offences, were the main reasons for the inception of the motoring organisations; this is rather different from the present-day concept of them as mainly assisting with breakdowns.

To determine the speed of a car, it was necessary to measure the time taken for it to cover a given distance. In 1903 the *Bury Free Press* reported that the Chief Constable of the West Suffolk Standing Joint Committee had asked for leave to purchase a dozen stop-watches at a cost of £10 10s (£10.50), for catching motorists. This was opposed by one member who stated, 'I hope they are not going to hide themselves and wait for motorists. It is perfectly disgraceful to think of policemen hiding behind a hedge catching them. It is un-English in every sense of the word.'

Measurements were usually taken over a minimum distance of one furlong. When the car passed the first policeman in hiding, he would signal to the second one at the

Punch *cartoon of 6 June 1906: 'A quiet Sunday in our village'. The dust problems were very real in summer. An advertisement for bijoux villas in Sudbury proclaimed they had roof gardens and freedom from motor dust. This cartoon shows a car being fettled by blacksmiths – a popular view. However, it was more likely to have been the cycle dealer who took an interest in motorised transport.*

9

end of the measured distance, and they would simultaneously start their stop-watches. A signal when the car passed the second policeman enabled two values of the elapsed time to be determined. A third policeman stopped the motorist while the times were compared with the minimum for the distance. The dust clouds created in the summer could make the observance of the second signal very difficult, giving justifiable concern over the accuracy of the speed.

Punch cartoons of the period reflected the general anxiety created by the new mode of transport. Fortunately, the relatively high cost of cars prevented them being seen in great numbers for many years, by which time road conditions had improved.

The Eastern Counties Automobile Club was formed in 1903, with its headquarters at the Great White Horse Hotel, Ipswich. The main objects of the club were 'to watch the progress, encourage and protect automobilism as much as possible; to afford members information and advice, and to make arrangements for lectures, discussions and tours; and to organise exhibitions and competitions'. The question of the legal defence of its members was of great interest, and it was finally agreed that 'it may undertake the defence of its members, but no legal action can be taken without the consent of a special general meeting'. The Earl of Stradbroke was the first President, with F. Bland as Chairman and Honorary Treasurer. The first annual subscription was £1 1s (£1.05).

The Club held runs to places as far away as Saxmundham, Bury St Edmunds and Diss. Several motorists would turn out, including Major Carthew of Woodbridge with a 10hp Wolseley, Mr Charles Castell of Wickham Market with a 10hp Rex, Mr J.R. Egerton in a 13hp Primus, Dr Rowe with a 5hp Peugeot, and Mr Vulliamy, the solicitor, on a BAT motorcycle. These runs were watched with great interest by large numbers of people along the route. The Club also held 'non-stop runs' (for example, Ipswich to Scole and back via Bungay and Beccles) where the cars were required to maintain a level pace without stopping their engines.

Another popular occasion was the motor gymkhana, held at Portman Road, Ipswich. Among the many exciting events to tempt participants were the egg and spoon race for motorcycles, the glass of water race, the tortoise race, the vegetable race, and musical cars – the highlight being the Turk's Head and pig-sticking competition. The reader will be spared details of these events.

In the west of the county, the *Bury Free Press* reported in 1903:

> . . . our local motorists are determined not to be behind the times with regard to an Automobile Club, and it was with this object in view that a meet of motorists was organised for Tuesday evening, on the Cornhill, Bury, whence a journey was made to Higham Railway Tavern, where a meeting was subsequently held. Mr Owen A. Clark on his 12hp Benz was accompanied by local dignitaries from the Church, and Police, and Mr T. H. Nice conveyed the representatives of the Press.

At a further meeting, Mr Moseley and Reggie Egerton from the Ipswich-based club were invited along, and they suggested that new clubs should be affiliated to the Eastern Counties Automobile Club, being the original one. This suggestion did not seem to be well received, and eventually the West Suffolk Automobile Club was

The Motor Car Act required that all drivers be licensed as from January 1904. Although Henry Lacy Scott held this licence, he was usually chauffeured by his sons.

No. **65**

MOTOR CAR ACT, 1903.

Administrative County of West Suffolk.

LICENCE TO DRIVE A MOTOR CAR (~~OR MOTOR CYCLE~~.)

Henry Lacy Scott of *87 Guildhall Street, Bury St. Edmund's*, is hereby licensed to drive a MOTOR CAR (~~or MOTOR CYCLE on~~ly) for the period of twelve months from the *first* day of *January 1904* until the *thirty-first* day of *December 1904* inclusive.

P. Townshend C. C.
Clerk to the County Council.

SHIRE HALL, BURY ST. EDMUND'S,
29th Dec. 1903.

N.B.—Particulars of any endorsement of any licence previously held by the person licensed must be entered on the back of this licence.

formed, with an impressive line-up of local dignitaries that the Ipswich Club would have envied:

President: The Right Hon. the Earl Cadogan KG
Vice-Presidents: Lord Iveagh, KP; Sir Henry Bunbury, Bart;
Sir T.G. Biddulph, Bart; The Hon. Walter Guinness

The future of the motor car was not a certainty in many people's minds, and even the converted were not always sure. At the Eastern Counties Club's first dinner, Mr Townsend Cobbold proclaimed, 'The expansion of motoring into a business matter in the county might come in time, and possibly the motor car might be the death of the light railway.'

The general development that had occurred in motoring since 1896 created pressure for a change to the Locomotives on Highways Act. New legislation was introduced in the Motor Car Act, 1903, which came into effect on 1 January 1904. Driving 'recklessly or negligently' was now an offence, and the maximum speed limit was raised to 20mph, after much debate. It remained at 12mph for heavy vehicles.

Annual driving licences were to be issued, and all vehicles were to be provided with a number and mark to indicate the registration council. The following marks were allocated for Suffolk:

East Suffolk	BJ
West Suffolk	CF
Ipswich	DX

The early registration details ought to be a source of useful information, but many have not survived. Nothing remains for West Suffolk from this early date. Some East Suffolk BJ registrations remain, but are in ring-binder form. Low numbers were sometimes transferred to a new car when the original one was sold, and the register shows that the BJ 1 plate, for example, belonged to Ranulphus Carthew of The Abbey, Woodbridge, with a 20hp Austin registered in 1920. This may well have been his third or fourth car to have the plate, as the previous registration details have not survived. The orders issued by the Local Government Board in November 1903 allowed local authorities to open their registers at once. East Suffolk was quick off the mark, as the earliest remaining car on the register is BJ 24, on 7 December 1903.

Fortunately, the original Ipswich County Borough Council's bound registration book survives, starting with DX 1, a 20hp Mercedes registered to William Pretty of Chandos House, Fonnereau Road, on 1 January 1904. He was a very keen motorist, along with his wife Mabel, who was the first woman to obtain a driving licence in Ipswich. The Mercedes followed an earlier Gobron Brillié, which was claimed to be the first car in Ipswich. When the time came to change his car, Mr Pretty was certainly not going to lose his precious registration, and subsequently he transferred it to a Minerva in 1911, and a 25hp Studebaker in 1913. A larger 40hp Mercedes was also acquired in 1908. The fee for transferring a number was £1.

The first registrations were seven years after the 'Emancipation Act' of 1896; therefore, they do not indicate the first cars used on the roads, as the year of manufacture or subsequent purchase are not recorded. (Appendices A and B show the first registrations and driving licences for Ipswich.) As all vehicles had to be registered for 1904, it does show the total number of cars and motorcycles in use at that time.

Ipswich County Borough Registrations for 1904
Total of motor cars and motorcycles: 109
Motor cars: 49%
Motor cycles: 51%

Car Manufacturer	Number	Country of Manufacture
De Dion	18	France
Darracq	10	France
Clement	5	France
Primus	3	Germany
Argyll	2	Scotland

The remaining 15 were all of different manufacture.

Although individual registrations do not exist for the rest of the county, the Ipswich data clearly show the influence of European manufacturers. Eighty per cent of all these cars originated in France. For 1905 the pattern changed, as 33 per cent of the new cars registered in Ipswich were of British manufacture, with names such as Enfield, Humber, Wolseley and Sunbeam.

The Autocar published details of the total number of county registrations, with the following being listed for Suffolk from January to mid-summer's day 1904.

Registrations from January to June 1904		
	Cars	Motorcycles
East Suffolk (BJ)*	101	101
West Suffolk (CF)	74	69
Ipswich (DX)	44	36

*The East Suffolk totals are correct, but the values were given as a combined number for cars and motorcycles, and were halved for compiling the table.

The chart below shows the variation in new registrations for the Ipswich County Borough Council between 1903 and 1919.

Combined Car and Motorcycle Registrations, Index letter DX

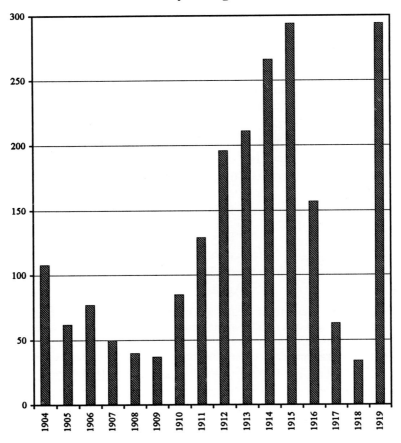

Cross Corner, Woodbridge. Horace Reynolds, or 'Poll' as he was known, appointed himself, without pay, as director of traffic at this notorious accident spot. After Poll died of pneumonia in 1910, Mr Palmer took up the position and is here conducting a car across the junction, c. 1912.

There were no white lines, traffic lights or stop signs at that time, and it was inevitable that collisions would occur where roads crossed. In 1901 Woodbridge Council fixed a mirror at the junction of Chapel Street and Market Hill in an attempt to avoid accidents. In the same town, Horace Reynolds, or 'Poll' as he was known, appointed himself, without pay, as the director of traffic at the 'Cross Corner'. He wore a red coat given to him by Lord Rendelsham, a flower-bedecked cap, and carried a flag. For nearly three years he performed this duty, preventing several accidents and becoming well-known to motorists over a wide area. In 1910, at the age of 32, he contracted pneumonia and died. His funeral caused a sensation, as the coffin was taken to the cemetery by motor car, a practice unheard of in the area at that time. As a tribute to him, a stone was erected with the following inscription:

To The Memory of
Horace Reynolds (Poll)
Who Died 22nd August, 1910
Aged 32 Years

Though lacking learning, or wealth, yet by his self-imposed task of watching
over the motor and other traffic at the Cross Corner in this town, in the course
of his duty preventing many serious mishaps, he proved himself a true helper
of his fellow men, and daily earned the gratitude not only of the townsfolk, but
also of all motorists and others who passed through the town.

A fatal accident occurred at the 'Cross Corner' only a few months later. Eventually Mr Palmer took up the job of traffic controller.

The Lamberts Almanacs for the period 1900–1917 provide considerable information from which the development of motorised transport can be gauged. (Appendix C gives motor-related excerpts from the annual review of important happenings in the county.) It soon becomes clear that accidents occurred from the earliest of times. However, these usually involved horses or pedestrians rather than other motorists, as in the following report.

> Mr Sansom manager of Brown and Co, timber merchants, was coming down the hill near Ufford Avenue on the main road, when the car skidded and ran into a brewer's dray with a pair of horses attached. The car hit the offside horse, which reared up and fell onto Mr Sansom who was sitting on the front seat of the car. When extricated, Mr Sansom was found to be dead, and the horse had to be shot.

The majority of non-motoring accidents listed for a year would relate to horse transport in some form, many being fatal.

During the early years of the century, the horsepower ratings were meant to relate to the actual engine output, although they were not usually very accurate. By 1907, the RAC method had been introduced, where the rated horsepower was solely a function of the bore and number of cylinders.

$$hp = \frac{d^2 x \; n}{2.5}$$

d = cylinder diameter in inches
n = number of cylinders

In later years, two figures would often be quoted for a car; for example, 14/40 – the first figure being the official RAC rating, the second the maximum horsepower at optimum engine speed.

It is often said that the first motor race occurred when two motorists met on the same stretch of road, as there has always been that urge to see whose vehicle is fastest. There was no official race-track in this country until the opening of Brooklands in 1907, and this was to remain the only one for many years. The situation might have been different if the wishes of Mawdsley Brooke had come true, as Suffolk would then have become the home of motor racing. His letter to *The Autocar* in 1901 read:

> There has been much discussion of late in reference to a motor car track or autodrome, but much of the difficulty seems in the choice of a suitable spot. Two miles from Lowestoft, at Oulton Broad, are some capital marshes, and always dry, and if a track were arranged there to run out by the river and back by the fringe of the marshes, a clear circuit of about 18 miles might be arranged, and variety obtained too. The run out to Beccles would be flat, but with plenty of gradual curves, and the run home could be arranged for rises, some of which would be natural. Above all, the cost of the ground should be reasonable; the distance from town is not great (100 miles), and Lowestoft is a good centre. All things considered, it is a spot that should receive attention when the time comes.

It was not to be, but from the earliest days, and throughout the country, local motoring clubs organised their own sprints and hill climbs, either on a short section of road

Lawford Hill near Manningtree, 1906. DX218 is a rare 24hp De Dion Bouton belonging to Roland Snowdon. The race report states that he was disqualified as his passengers interfered with the driving!

or perhaps the driveway of a country house. The Ipswich and East Suffolk Automobile Club (the Eastern Counties Automobile Club until December 1905) was instrumental in organising such events at various locations. In 1906 they held a climb at Lawford Hill near Manningtree, timed on an average 1 in 10 hill, over a distance of 760 yards. The local authorities assisted by repairing and watering the track prior to the event. The following competitors took part:

J.R. Egerton	16hp Humber
F. Scottorn	14hp Hallamshire
Lindsay Scott	10hp Lindsay
C.R. Garrard	12hp Clement Talbot
Dr E.L. Rowe	10/12hp Humber
Dr Pringle	8/10hp Humber
Mr Hackblock	24hp Hallamshire
W.M. Cooke	15hp Darracq
C. Castell	12hp Clement Talbot
Mr Kirby	12hp Orleans
Dr Hossack	10hp Alldays
Dr Moseley	6hp De Dion
Dr Brown	12hp Hallamshire
Colonel Davis	16hp De Dietrich
A. Alston	6hp Swift

The winner of this 'doctors' convention' was Dr Moseley, with the smallest car. One of the entrants, C.R. Garrard, was a designer of engines for the British-built

Talbots, one of which he was driving. Often a very complex handicap system was set up for these events and, surprisingly for the period, an electrical timing system was in use. Devised by Mr Scottorn, this consisted of tapes on the ground at the start and finish, connected by wires to electromagnets which operated the stop-watches.

For 1907 the venue was changed to private land, with standing-mile and flying-kilometre events being held at Sudbourne Hall, Orford. Two Suffolk-built cars were entered in this event and driven by their makers: Mawdsley Brooke set the fastest time of the day in his 30/35hp Brooke, with 1 minute 10 seconds for the flying mile, and Lindsay Scott in his Woodbridge-built 15hp Lindsay won his own class. Charles Castell, the agent for Talbot cars in Wickham Market, achieved a speed of 56.16mph in the flying-kilometre class with his two-cylinder 10/12hp model.

A year later, Hascot Hill, between Battisford and Barking, was the location, with a maximum 1 in 6 gradient. The big disappointment was the non-appearance of William Pretty with his new Mercedes, due to a 'slight mishap'. In the same year, speed trials were held on Lord Rendlesham's estate in Rendlesham Park. From Eyke Gate to the Hall there was an almost straight drive of 1.25 miles, which enabled both standing-mile and flying-kilometre classes to be held. Lord Rendlesham joined in the spirit of the occasion by entering his Alldays, but was unable to compete due to 'unavoidable causes'. Marion Hackblock cleaned up the Ladies Class, being the only contestant, while Garrard's 25hp Talbot took the trade class, covering the mile in 1 minute 20.6 seconds. Tea was served in the marquee during the interval.

In Suffolk, some indication of the growth of the motor trade can be gained from county directories such as Kelly's. For 1896 there is no reference to the motor car, but by 1900 two firms are listed: W. Youngs of Lowestoft, a motor car proprietor, and the Anglian Cycle & Engineering Co Ltd in Stowmarket, listed under motor car manu-facturers. (Appendix D gives details of firms up to 1912.) There were certainly other firms involved in motoring activities who were not included in the directories, and many may have been in business for some time before having an entry, but never-theless it shows the general pattern of rapid expansion.

The first decade of this century saw mainly the well-off owning motor cars. Although the younger ones were eager to get behind the wheel themselves, their parents were more likely to have needed the services of a chauffeur. But who would teach the chauffeur to drive?

Mr Adams of the 'St John' Cycle and Motor Works in Woodbridge advertised that they were able to supply any make of new car, and would also teach your chauffeur to drive. However, the majority were probably self-taught, with the knowledge of repair skills being a prime requirement.

Alfred Adams started his 'St John' Cycle depot from a converted house in the Thoroughfare in 1902. The business flourished, and he was soon selling his 'St John' motorcycles, along with cars and a great number of bicycles. By 1909, larger premises were needed and he moved to the old 'Foundry', which he converted into a cycle and motor works and garage. His advertisements had a certain flair to them and established him as the main person in the area to contact for cars, motorcycles and bicycles. He

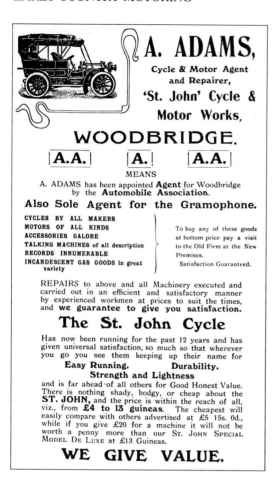

Alfred Adams' 1910 advertisement still placed emphasis on bicycle sales, even though he was an AA agent.

also took on another line as sole agent for 'His Master's Voice' gramophones and other talking machines. This was a common sideline to boost trade during the winter months, when motor vehicles were less in use.

By around 1910, the popularity of the car was increasing, and it became cheaper to run than a horse and carriage. Contemporary figures gave a cost of 5.33d per mile (2.2p) for the average car, compared with 9.94d (4.1p) for a horse and carriage.

Towards the end of the first decade the car was becoming more accepted, but higher speeds and the dust problem were still causing difficulties. Although the general speed limit was 20mph, the Local Government Board had powers to adopt lower limits if appropriate. In November 1908, the Local Government Board held an enquiry at the Workhouse in Wickham Market, where the East Suffolk County Council applied for a 10mph limit on the main road. A large number of people attended, including several prominent motorists. The application was opposed by J.W. Gordon Steward (Hon. Secretary of Ipswich and East Suffolk Automobile Club), C.D. Castell, J.W. Orde (Secretary of the RAC), J. Stuart Ogilvie JP, and W. Rees Jeffreys (Secretary of the Motor Union). The inspector asked for a show of hands, and there were 40–50 for and 6 against. Wickham Market got its 10mph limit, and Mr Read, Clerk of the Parish

Council, was presented with a Westminster Clock by voluntary subscription, in recognition of the able way he had conducted the parish's case.

The new limit was enforced by the local police, and in 1909 a man from Surrey was charged with driving a motor car at a speed dangerous to the public. The claimed speed was 50mph. In this case, the police method used varied from that described earlier in this chapter. Posts were set up at the beginning and end of the 10mph limit, a distance of 1,609 yards, with no visual contact – clearly impossible under these conditions! The procedure started with the comparing of watches. A policeman at either end of the town would then record the time and registration number of each vehicle that passed him, and a third policeman would stop the drivers to take details and advise them that they had been through a trap. At the end of the session, all the elapsed times would be calculated and any offending motorist notified. It is interesting to record that twenty-two cars passed through the town in three hours, a rare indicator of the volume of traffic on a main road in those days. When the case came before the local magistrates, the defendant's lawyer argued that as the roads were deserted, the speed could not be considered dangerous to the public, and that his client was not actually being charged with exceeding the speed limit. The magistrates were not impressed and fined the defendant £1, with 18s (90p) costs.

Timings made in this way could not have been very accurate as they effectively relied on one calculated time rather than two averaged results from stop-watches. Over a three-hour period, there could be a variation in basic time between the two watches, with readings from a minute hand giving further tolerance. The policeman stated that the defendant passed him '*about 2.15*'.

An interesting trio in Charles Austin's stableyard at Brandeston Hall. From the left: a 1908 Sizaire Naudin, a 1908 De Dion Bouton, and a Mercedes-like tourer with detachable brougham top.

Frank Burrell opened these premises on Angel Hill, Bury St Edmunds, in 1907. His advertisement claimed it was the 'Best garage in Bury', with cars to let from 3 guineas a day. The cars on view here are, from the left, a Gladiator, c. 1905; a 6hp Panhard with an Elswick body; a 6hp Wolseley, c. 1905; a Gladiator, c. 1905; and a 16/20hp Beeston Humber, c. 1905.

Wickham Market had started the trend for lower speed limits, and Woodbridge UDC made a similar application in 1909. Ipswich was to follow in 1912, but there was more opposition here as it was claimed that the congestion in the town would not be eased by a lower speed, and would in fact be made worse. No record has been found to indicate that the Local Government Board considered this application.

The rising use and popularity of the motor car was soon to be dashed by the outbreak of war with Germany. The general pattern of austerity at home meant that private motoring all but stopped, and this decline was further accelerated by the press who wrote long articles about the selfish motorist. There was a national appeal in 1916 to stop the use of cars for pleasure.

Petrol licences were issued for business purposes, and eventually motoring taxes were all severely increased, with the end result that many cars were laid up until the end of hostilities. In 1914 Reggie Egerton was summoned for keeping 300 gallons of petrol in the grounds of his house in Rushmere Road, Ipswich. The police had found a hundred tins of No 1 Shell, and fifty of No 2 Shell hidden under garden refuse behind his house. He claimed that the petrol was being kept for the Government, and that he had no intention of holding up prices as he would normally sell it at the market price of 1s 9d (8.75p). He also claimed that some dealers were taking advantage of the situation and selling at 10s (50p) a gallon. The Bench decided that he was guilty of an offence under the Petroleum Act of 1871, seized the petrol and fined him £4, with 2 guineas (£2.10) costs.

Zeppelin raids over the English coast saw the introduction of the Defence of the Realm Regulations. The 'Order as to Lights' was issued in Bury St Edmunds in January 1915 and, apart from general blackout requirements, prohibited the use of powerful lights on motors in areas of reduced street lighting.

These Orders were not strictly enforced until Bury received its first raid in April 1915. Fortunately there was no loss of life, but considerable damage was caused to many properties, with fire spreading to T. H. Nice & Co's motor and cycle shop on the Buttermarket. Any private motoring was now very much in decline, and it was mainly military vehicles that were seen on the roads, particularly in Bury St Edmunds.

Motoring firms were generally reliant on commercial and military work where available, but many would turn their hand to any area of employment. Larger companies such as Botwoods fulfilled orders for military vehicles by converting cars into trucks. There was an obvious need for ambulances, which was often met by adding suitable coachwork to a car.

The Government had requested the formation of a Motor Volunteer Corps, and in March 1918 the Suffolk Corps was inaugurated. Local sections were also formed, such as the one at Framlingham. A meeting of some fifty drivers at the Crown Hotel saw Captain Richard Carley elected officer in charge, with the task of organising vehicles so they could reach the battle lines as quickly as possible.

The war gave many men their first opportunity to be involved with various forms of motor transport, and if they were fortunate enough to return, they were usually keen to carry on motoring.

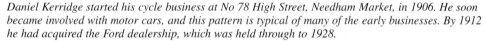

Daniel Kerridge started his cycle business at No 78 High Street, Needham Market, in 1906. He soon became involved with motor cars, and this pattern is typical of many of the early businesses. By 1912 he had acquired the Ford dealership, which was held through to 1928.

Cadillac V8 on the Market Hill, Framlingham. This type of car was extensively used for the transport of senior personnel during the First World War. It was the first V8 car to achieve commercial success and was renowned for its quality. Cadillac were the first to fit electric starting and lighting as standard.

CHAPTER TWO

PRACTICAL MOTORING

During the early years of motoring, when most people had little knowledge of mechanical matters, the options and potential problems were far greater than they are today. This chapter looks at some of the issues that affected the motorist before the First World War.

The basic means of propulsion was certainly not limited to the internal combustion engine. In the early years of this century, steam cars were popular, with makes such as the Stanley, the Pearson-Cox, the White and the Locomobile. Although there was considerable knowledge of steam power at that time, these cars eventually lost their appeal because of concerns over explosions, complexity and cost.

Glencairn Stuart Ogilvie was a keen devotee, and in 1901 was converted to the pleasures of a Gardner-Serpollet steamer after many disastrous experiences with normal petrol-engined cars. Referring to the latter he said, 'I was so disheartened that I confess I was within an ace of returning to my old love, and sticking to horse flesh for the rest of my natural existence.' He was later to become very involved with motoring inventions, but is best remembered for his development of Thorpeness as a holiday village.

Early steamers such as the Locomobile were fairly basic, and required frequent stops for water. Hubert Egerton drove one from John O'Groats to Land's End in December 1900, and calculated that he had put over five tons of water into the car. The petrol burner often blew out, and he described the journey as 'rather like sitting on a garden seat, with no more protection than was provided by one's overcoat, while the garden seat wandered along through rain, sleet, snow and gale, at anything between 10 and 20mph'.

J. Vincent, in his book *Through East Anglia In A Motor Car*, describes trips taken in 1906 in various cars. On one of these ventures, in an 18hp White steam car, he was accompanied by Frederick Coleman, London manager of the White Steam Car Company of the United States, their wives, one child and a mechanic. The fuel was petrol or benzolene and between three and five minutes were required to raise steam before the car could move off. It would then need to be filled with water every 150 miles or so. Vincent was most impressed by the steamer, particularly after it had crossed from Felixstowe to Bawdsey on the steam ferry.

We were faced with the stiffest task I have ever seen offered to any motor car, in the shape of a sharply sloping bank of soft gravel to be ascended without any preliminary run of any kind. The steam car, however, ploughed slowly through the gravel and up the hill, and I look back upon those ten or twelve yards of hill climbing as the finest exhibition of sheer strength in a motor car it has ever been my fortune to witness.

On his local motoring exploits, Vincent enjoyed the use of several different cars, one being a Rolls Royce driven by Claude Johnson, an important figure within that well-known company. Vincent stresses that he had no connection with any of the manufacturers of these cars, but the lack of any mechanical malfunction might suggest that the chosen vehicles had been well prepared beforehand, particularly when you consider who the owners were. Motoring books of the time were, of course, trying to portray a positive image of this new form of transport, and you could hardly expect these trips to be a catalogue of disasters.

On one occasion, though, Mr Coleman was not entirely happy with the behaviour of the White steamer they were using, and thoughtfully telegraphed to London for another one, which awaited them on arrival at their hotel in Ipswich.

Another form of motive power was the electric motor, but its weakness, which remains to this day, was the problem of how to provide a battery of adequate capacity. People were very impressed by the smooth, quiet running of these cars, but disappointed at their lack of range. The electric motor, therefore, was no competition for

Steam power was a serious alternative to the internal combustion engine in the early years of the century. Members of the Woodbridge Social Book Club arrive in an American White steam car to celebrate the centenary of the town's famous poet, Edward Fitzgerald, in 1909. By this time, however, the popularity of steam was fading.

Hubert Egerton, older brother of Reggie, was nationally known for his pioneering feats. His De Dion Bouton quadricycle of c. 1899 is well prepared for another motoring adventure.

the internal combustion engine, which soon began to dominate, even though there was originally no infrastructure to provide it with fuel.

The London firm of Carless, Capel & Leonard promoted the name 'petrol' for a refined spirit they were using in motor launches. The very earliest motorist would have resorted to other fuels and there was often much confusion over the various types available. Even when petrol was introduced, motorists still had to locate somewhere to buy it. Suppliers would often include chemists, ironmongers and public houses, as well as the more obvious bicycle and motor firms. For example, John Betts, a dispensing chemist in Woodbridge, proudly stated in his 1904 advertisement that in addition to supplying trusses, enemas and elastic rubber goods, he was an agent for petrol. And in 1905 Shell announced that their petrol could be obtained from the following outlets:

J.A. Sturton Ltd, sole wholesale agent for distribution, 9 Falcon Street, Ipswich
Warren & Co, 95 London Road, Ipswich
Hillyard & Co, Princes Street, Ipswich
Mr Hammond, St Nicholas Street, Ipswich
Kettle & Co, Brook Street, Ipswich

Mr Hubert, Felixstowe Road, Ipswich
Mr Boon, 17 Crown Street, Ipswich
Mr Garrard, Cycle Agent, Needham Market
The Victoria Hardware Stores, The Parade, Felixstowe
Mr Crisp, Cycle Works, Walton, Nr Felixstowe
Mr Money, Orwell Road, Felixstowe
Mr Potter, Needham Market

Nowadays, the risk of not being able to find a petrol station is so small that most motorists do not carry a can in the boot. However, in the first years of the century, outlets were very few and far between, even on the main roads. As with most things in life, where there is a need, somebody will be prepared to supply it. One such enterprising person was Robert Plant, landlord of the famous Magpie at Stonham Parva on the Ipswich to Norwich road. His son Bob recalled playing marbles, bowling hoops, and playing various games on the 'turnpike' with no fear of being run over. The occasional car would stop at the pub, not only for the refreshment of the occupants, but because it was one of the very first places on that road to sell petrol. The pub ledgers, which still exist, record not only the beer sales but also those of 'Carburine' motor spirit, from 1s 2d (approximately 6p) a gallon.

Conveying petrol to these retail outlets still relied on the traditional methods: in fact, it was delivered by the very transport that the car was trying to replace. In the Framlingham area, a horse and wagon brought the green Pratts petrol cans from the Anglo American Oil Company depot in Wickham Market. These sealed cans each held two gallons, and the petrol sold for 2s (10p) a gallon, and the can itself cost 3s (15p).

This advertisement, c. 1905, shows cans of petrol for sale stacked on the pavement. Note the diversity of products being sold by a cycle dealer who was also moving into the motor trade.

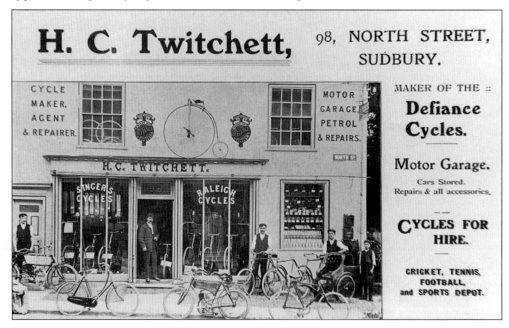

Anglo American Oil Company, Sudbury Station, c. 1925. On the left is a Model T Ford, adjacent to the larger Pierce Arrow. This location is now a car park, but the Great Eastern Hotel still exists. In earlier days, before specialised lorries were developed, petrol was distributed by horse and wagon.

The empty can would then be exchanged for a full one. Later on, the petrol was delivered in 40-gallon drums on the back of a lorry, prior to the development of purpose-made tankers.

Leslie Kerridge remembered the early days of his father's motor business in Needham Market, when petrol cans were kept in a locked pit at the bottom of the garden. A round trip, from the customer on the pavement, through the house and garden to the pit and back with funnel and measure again, was not much fun in winter. They also provided an important service by delivering petrol to local customers. The prudent motorist had to ensure that he kept sufficient supplies on the car and at home, as retail outlets were few, and invariably closed when needed.

Petrol has always presented a fire risk, and as early as 1904 the Cresswell Motor Car Stores in Newmarket were completely destroyed, along with six or seven cars. The damage was estimated at between £1,000 and £2,000. On another occasion, a car belonging to Sir Cuthbert Quilter caught fire in the Buttermarket, Ipswich, but, fortunately, Lady Quilter had just alighted and nobody was hurt. Botwood & Egerton were quick to see the sales potential of this hazard and promptly placed large advertisements in the *EADT* for car fire extinguishers at £2 2s (£2.10) each.

Motorists have always been concerned about fuel consumption figures, and in 1906 members of the Ipswich and East Suffolk Automobile Club carried out their own fuel consumption trials. They were carried out over a 50-mile run from Ipswich to Marks Tey and back, with the results being determined from the weight of the car in pounds, divided by the number of ounces of spirit used. Charles Castell from Wickham Market in his Clement Talbot was first, with a consumption that worked out at 57 miles per gallon. Reggie Egerton, who also took part in the trial, considered that a mistake must have been made, as the previous record was 38.1mpg. He aired his views on the matter in the local newspapers, much to the annoyance of fellow members who in turn wrote letters to state how carefully all the tests had been performed, and that the result must stand. The final outcome is not recorded, but Reggie's intuition may have been right.

Problems due to blockages by dirt in the fuel pipe were fairly common. Vincent had some practical advice on this matter. To avoid getting petrol in the mouth while trying to clear a blockage, he advocated the use of an idle bystander to blow the pipe for you, and suggested a shilling (5p) recompense for a boy, and half a crown (12.5p) for a man, 'especially if he is large and rough'.

The majority of cars in the first two decades of this century were of the open type, which necessitated the driver and passengers being well dressed to combat the elements. Firms responded well to this requirement, and a wide range of protective clothing was available. A contemporary booklet, *Motoring in East Anglia,* gave the following advice:

> It is well to be prepared for the lowering of temperature that comes with swift passage through the air, so that clothing a good deal warmer than you would require for walking should be worn. Ladies accompanying the party should be implored to observe this precaution, and to wear head gear which will not require constant attention to keep it in place. Often an otherwise pleasant holiday tour has been spoilt by the evident discomfort of the ladies of the party, whose one idea at the beginning was to look smart, whereas after a few miles one would generally prefer to be comfortable rather than smart. It is undoubtedly possible to be both comfortable and smart; but this necessitates warm clothing and small close fitting hats. For those who desire to put up at good-class hotels, it is advisable to carry a change of dress for dinner.

Before venturing onto the road, various legal procedures had to be followed: a driving licence had to be obtained at a cost of 5s (25p), the car had to be registered with the county borough or council (£1), and registration plates had to be fitted. From 1909 it was also necessary to obtain a taxation licence known as the Road Fund Tax. This was on a sliding scale depending on calculated horsepower.

Road Fund Tax		
Motorcycles and tricycles	£ 1	
Motor cars not exceeding 6.5hp	£ 2 2s	(£ 2.10)
6.5–12hp	£ 3 3s	(£ 3.15)
12–16hp	£ 4 4s	(£ 4.20)
16–26hp	£ 6 6s	(£ 6.30)
26–33hp	£ 8 8s	(£ 8.40)
33–40hp	£10 10s	(£10.50)
40–60hp	£21	(£21.00)
over 60hp	£42	(£42.00)

A delightful photograph showing that motoring was not an exclusively male pursuit. Suitable protection against the weather was always essential, and a wide range of motoring clothing was available. The car is an 8hp Model 0 De Dion Bouton of c. 1903–4.

Also, if you had a chauffeur, you would need to apply to the Inland Revenue for a licence to keep a male servant, at a cost of 15s (75p). Insurance was not compulsory then, but the wise motorist would have taken out some form of cover.

It was advisable to load up the car with a vast array of equipment before starting a journey, and one early guide recommended taking the following, as a minimum.

Accessories, tools and spares for ordinary journeys:
Accumulator; jack; aprons and rugs; lamps; burner for acetylene lamps; magneto contacts and points; carbide; nuts, bolts and washers; contact breaker; blade and screw; oil; engine valves and springs; two oil cans; files (round and flat); petrol in 2-gallon tin; feeler gauges; pliers; grease and injector; screwdrivers; hammer; spanners to fit all nuts; hand vice; spare wheel; horn; sparking plugs; inner tubes; split pins; insulating tape; spring washers and straps; twine and cord; voltmeter; tyre inflator; washers; tyre levers; wire (copper 16g, iron 20g and 30g, and high tension); tyre repair outfit; tyre valves; wrenches.

Additional equipment for long runs:
Brass polish; lamp parts; cleaning brushes; gloves; leathers; cloths and waste; maps; overalls; extra spare tyre; engine oil; foot muffs in winter; trembler for coil; hacksaw; vulcaniser.

Having piled all this equipment into the car, it would then be necessary to check the petrol via a dip stick, if no gauge were fitted. Starting the engine would be difficult until the knack was mastered, and there are many tales relating to injuries caused by the starting handle. The idea of a self-starting mechanism was well established although not much used at that time. As with so many aspects of early motoring, several methods were tried.

When running, the engine would wind a large spring on the crankshaft. On restarting, the spring would be activated from the driver's seat, giving the engine a few turns. Hopefully, it would then start; if not, it was back to the crank. The explosion starter consisted of an external pump (hand-operated), which pumped acetylene gas into each cylinder via non-return valves. This method had to be used with an ignition system that would cause a spark when turned on, causing combustion in one cylinder, followed by the next two or three, which should have been sufficient for it to fire normally on petrol.

Another alternative was to have a compressed-air cylinder. This was charged by a small gear-driven compressor when the engine was running. To start the engine, the air was led to a distributor and then to each cylinder, causing the crankshaft to rotate. The engine would then fire when the air was cut off and the throttle opened. An advantage of this system was that it could also be used to pump up tyres.

The present form of electric starter was in its infancy at this time, but would eventually surpass the more exciting methods described above.

Having coaxed the engine into life and manipulated the throttle and ignition levers on the steering wheel, it was time to move off. As well as being aware of the road conditions, it was necessary to drive in a thoughtful manner so as to avoid undue strain on the braking system and tyres, which still holds true today.

The law required a car to have two brakes, and one of these would often be on the rear wheel, with the other on the transmission shaft. Front-wheel braking did not develop much prior to the First World War as problems with the steering and suspension had yet to be overcome.

It is not surprising, then, that one of the greatest fears of the early motorist was sideslip. This phenomenon was likely to occur when braking on any wet or greasy surface, as it is akin to pulling on the handbrake in a modern car. The problem was compounded by the tyres, which had minimal tread patterns and were inflated to very high pressures, varying between 45 and 80 pounds per square inch, depending on load and section.

To minimise the evils of sideslip, it was recommended that motorists drove on the crown of the road as much as possible, and that one of the front tyres should have a tread pattern. The accessory manufacturer proliferated even in those days, and there were many non-skid devices that could be fitted over tyres.

Stopping on hills is never easy, and is even more difficult without a good hand-brake. The early option for overcoming this problem was the sprag, or 'devil', a spiked rod hinged to the underside of the car. On coming to a halt, a lever was pulled which lowered the sprag and dug itself into the ground, preventing backward movement. Needless to say, this device could have disastrous consequences if applied while moving backwards at any speed.

Following the advice to drive on the crown of the road meant that some form of audible warning was necessary and, once again, the options were endless. The bulb and electric horn are familiar to us today, but the exhaust whistle is not. Although it could play some pleasant tunes, it was not effective in an emergency as the engine would be decelerating and therefore not producing sufficient gas to operate the whistle. The electric klaxon horn was far more effective, but was not recommended for use near cyclists or horses due to the terrifying noise it produced. It was ideal when overtaking traction engines, though. Noise could also be made with a gong, which was struck by hammers fixed to the cooling fan.

Speedometers were not a legal requirement until 1927, but they were very useful as a means of controverting any suggestions of speeding.

Lighting systems were fairly basic, often with a combination of oil lamps on the side and rear, with electric or acetylene gas for the main lamps. Ignition was primarily by battery and coil, which meant dependence on a battery for starting the engine. Nowadays, charging a battery is fairly straightforward, but how did early motorists manage before the wonders of electricity reached them? They simply made their own accumulators to do the job. Morgan Watts remembered the construction of such a device. First of all, a large non-porous bowl was needed; water and sulphuric acid were then added until a specific gravity of 1.28 was achieved. A further two pots were then required, one inside the other, with the inside one being porous. Next was a trip to the chemist to buy some micromate of potash, which would be ground up in a coffee grinder and added. Zinc sticks were wired up and put in the pots, using mercury as a liquid conductor. The output from the accumulator was then used to charge the 6-volt batteries. It was no wonder that most people preferred to stay with their well loved, clean, quiet and easy-starting horses.

Navigation by night was difficult, due to the poor lighting and road conditions, and if the location was unknown, the trip was better not attempted at all. Reggie Egerton was able to take such difficulties in his stride, and described a 180-mile journey that he undertook on a Century tandem in July 1900, starting at 5 o'clock in the afternoon. He arrived in time for breakfast the next day, but his average speed was pulled down by numerous halts – to ask the way or climb up signposts to shine a light. Such exploits were not for the faint hearted, who would have taken the train or stayed at home.

Vincent found night driving a 'trying experience to the nerves and to the eyes', and resolved to avoid it unless the moon was strong. His first journey in darkness was from Bury St Edmunds to Ipswich. Starting off with oil lamps only, it soon became necessary to use the acetylene lamps, but even they were not effective, particularly in the misty patches. He concluded that this type of driving was not to be recommended.

Mawdsley Brooke at the wheel of his own three-cyclinder Brooke, which won its class in the 1903 1,000 Miles Trial for absence of dust. Cars were required to drive over a 60-yard patch of white flour so that judges could determine their dust-raising capabilities.

For the stranger, matters were not much improved in the daytime. The increased mobility of people nowadays makes us forget how insular communities were at the turn of the century. Life revolved around the village and there was little call to go further. The person who needed to ask directions was often treated with suspicion as he was obviously from foreign parts.

There were usually no village signs as everybody was familiar with where they lived, and a stranger in a large town such as Ipswich would be even worse off, owing to the congestion in the streets and uncertainty over directions. Vincent, in his first journey out of Ipswich in 1906, attempted to overcome this problem by taking on a passenger who claimed to know the area well. No doubt he did when on foot, but the greater speed of the 15hp Panhard meant much indecision and backtracking. Vincent's impression of Ipswich was not too favourable: he complained of narrow streets, the juggernaut mood of the electric trams, and the inability to draw up at the kerbside. The police upset him by not allowing his car to stop outside the Great White Horse Hotel, even for unloading. He was probably viewed as a typical motorist of the time – someone with lots of money and a new toy. The average person could not have afforded a car, yet alone the services of a chauffeur and mechanic which he considered necessary for these journeys.

The rapid expansion of the railway network in mid-Victorian times meant that the road system had become very neglected, and it was certainly not ready for the onslaught of the motor car. The roads were unmade and generally in poor condition, with holes being filled with stones. The *Bury Free Press,* in 1899, commented on the disgraceful road conditions: 'The fact is undisputable that our Suffolk roads are a reproach to the County.' It went on to recommend the use of granite and a steam roller. A letter in the *EADT* for January 1903 followed a similar theme:

> The criticisms of your various correspondents upon the conditions of our roads are quite justified. I have also for years, driven over three and part of four counties termed Eastern, and I confirm that Suffolk roads are the worst of the lot. Look, during wet weather at two main roads, approaches to the borough of Ipswich itself, Woodbridge and Spring roads are usually in a fearful state, and footpaths past description. Do you see that state of things in main road approaches to Norwich, Colchester, Chelmsford or Cambridge? Nay! a thousand times nay! I am etc.

> Another traveller

By 1906, Vincent found little had changed as he entered the county from Scole. He was full of praise for the Norfolk roads but, on entering Suffolk, found the surfaces far worse than any previously encountered, along with illegible and tumbledown milestones. He commented that 'despite anti-skid gaiters, there was no hold for the wheels in the dirty porridge-like mud, concealing a crumbling sub-surface'. Morgan Watts recalled the A12, or 'turnpike' as it was known in the first decade of the century, when a large dust cloud would signal the approach of a motor car from a long way off. When the car did appear, the driver would be well protected from the elements, with goggles on and a very dirty face.

For the non-motoring public, the dust created by the passage of a car was a very real problem – it penetrated houses, dirtied the washing, and was a general nuisance. It was felt that the design of a car could influence the amount of dust raised, and manufacturers were keen to minimise this effect. The 1,000 Miles Trial of 1903 had a section where the competitors had to drive over a 60-yard patch of white flour so the judges could determine their dust-raising capabilities. The Lowestoft-manufactured Brooke car won its class, with 445 out of 500 marks for absence of dust.

It was obviously better to tackle the problem at source by improving the road surface, and many ideas were tried. Dr Rowe of the Borough Asylum in Ipswich was a keen motorist and owner of a 5hp Peugeot, registration DX12. He reported in 1909 that a number of experiments had been made to dampen the dust with both water-gas tar and calcium chloride, and, so far as he could see, both methods were very successful. The problem, however, would not disappear for good until the tarmac surface became commonplace.

The *'Contour' Road Book of England,* 1912, listed many of the main roads, with descriptions of their general condition. The Ipswich to Yarmouth section did not receive a very favourable report.

Considering that this is the London road, the surface is very poor. From Ipswich to Saxmundham, the surface is generally good, but there are frequent places where it is somewhat loose. From Saxmundham into Yarmouth the road is somewhat sandy, and there are a great many loose stones. The road may be said to be alternately good and bad.

It was not surprising that punctures were frequent, and 3,000 miles from a tyre was considered good. Mawdsley Brooke was pleased to have covered over 1,260 miles with no trouble, and his testimony was used by Dunlop in their advertisement of 1903.

Dear Sir,
I feel I must write and tell you of the satisfactory way in which the set of Dunlop tyres fitted to my car No 68, 14hp Brooke, have carried me through the 1,000 Miles reliability trials.

Previous to the trials, these tyres had run 260 miles, and I have had absolutely no trouble whatever with them, and honestly they now look almost as well as when I started, showing no sign of wear. I must congratulate you on at last having produced a satisfactory tyre suitable for heavy cars.
Yours truly

Mawdsley Brooke

Glencairn Stuart Ogilvie of Sizewell Hall invented an alternative to the pneumatic tyre, which he called the Vieo wheel. This consisted of a number of cylindrical rubbers located between solid inner and outer rims, and is here fitted to the rear wheels of his 24hp Napier. An endurance trial in 1906 had to be halted after damage to the wheels. Note the sprag located below the drive chain, which was lowered to prevent a car rolling backwards.

John Balfour Rainy, with his immaculate Argyll at Keddington, 1906. The covered spare tyre is a 'Stepney' wheel (named after a street in Llanelli), consisting of a tyre, tube and rim. This was clamped to the wheel in the event of a puncture. Argylls were manufactured in Scotland between 1899 and 1932.

Not everyone saw the pneumatic tyre as the ultimate choice for road wheels, and Glencairn Stuart Ogilvie was one of those who pursued alternatives. He invented the Vieo wheel, which consisted of two concentric rims between which were located cylindrical rubber isolators. These provided resilience without direct contact with the ground. He sold the patent and in 1905 became a director of a new company promoting them. The following year saw much publicity, with the Vieo wheels on Mr Stuart Ogilvie's Daimler being entered in a 4,000-mile trial under the competition rules of the ACGBI. After 2,676 miles, the trial was halted as all the rubber sections were damaged and there were fractures in the outer rim. It would seem that the considerable number of parts to the system, and the impact to which they were subjected, would inevitably lead to significant maintenance costs. Stuart Ogilvie was not deterred, though, and commercially launched the Vieo wheel in 1909, by which time the pneumatic tyre was well developed.

J.W. Brooke & Co also constructed a compensated spring wheel device, based on the designs of Arthur Robinson from Beccles. Such inventions, when viewed from the end of this century, may seem rather comical, but at the time were seen as an alternative to the problems of the pneumatic tyre.

Mending punctures was no easy task as the early wheels were not detachable. The wheel had to be jacked up and the tyre and tube removed in situ – a difficult and dirty job, particularly on a muddy roadside. Some cars had a separate rim and tyre called a

'Stepney' wheel, which could be bolted to the outside of the wheel until the tyre was changed later.

As tyres were very expensive, there was a necessity to mend rather than replace them. Often as not, the treads would still be in good condition but there would be a bad gash in the casing caused by a sharp flint. When this happened, Morgan Watts would cut off the edge beads and then make up a patch from a piece of external belting, as used on stationary engines. This would be stretched over the tyre and held in place with the belt clips.

Problems with tyres were common in the early days. Here Reggie Egerton displays the technique for removing and replacing the inner tube on his 8.5hp Decauville, with the wheel on the axle, in 1901. Detachable wheels were not available before about 1905 and a knowledge of tyre repairs was essential for even the shortest journey.

Alfred Garnham had one of the earliest garages in Ipswich and promoted it as a centre for tyre repair work. His advertisement stated: 'Largest retreading plant in Eastern Counties. Covers of any size rerubberised and rebuilt on the premises. First in 1897, foremost in 1906.'

In an emergency, if the tyre was ruined, one recommendation was to remove the inner tube and stuff the cover with hay! Victor Brewster recalled that as a young boy in around 1905, his father hired a car to take the family out for the day. On the return journey from Ingham to Long Melford, a puncture occurred, which was remedied by fitting the 'Stepney' wheel. Before long, though, the car had a second puncture, and the only option was to collect grass and vegetation from the roadside and stuff it in the cover. This enabled them to complete the journey, but the tyre and contents were in a sad state on reaching their destination.

It was also possible to buy kits to convert the hub centre so that it could be easily unbolted for quicker wheel changes.

The question of reliability in early motoring is a difficult one to assess, as recorded comments will often highlight the extremes. The following reports are typical, but much would have depended on the type and age of car, and the mileage covered.

Mr George Arnott of Woodbridge recalled the experience of his uncle, the Reverend Arthur Robbs, who, having been offered the living of a Norfolk parish near Stoke Ferry, decided to visit it by motor car. Accompanied by Mr Gall, the Reverend Titcombe, Chaplain of Seckford Hospital, and his brother, he set off at 8.30am one spring day in 1907. At 3pm, within three quarters of a mile of their destination, the car broke down and they had to walk the rest of the way. After the car had been repaired at the village smithy, it was decided not to return home that night but to stop at Thetford. Next morning, the intrepid travellers were early on their way, but after more breakdowns and punctures they finally abandoned the car outside Stowmarket and returned home by train.

As expected, Reggie Egerton's view was more optimistic, and he recorded these comments in the 1950s:

> Between 1902 and 1905 there were any number of really good cars, which did yeoman service in the hands of the public, and when 1912 was reached, I well remember a certain 12hp four-cylinder Wolseley which was so very well designed and so soundly constructed that I wondered how ever it could possibly be improved.

Charles Garrard bought a 14–16hp Argyll for hire work in 1909. A year later he set out from Framlingham on a fourteen-day tour of Wales and the Lake District. His receipts show that the car was garaged every night and 48 gallons of petrol were bought in total, over a distance of 944 miles. The only other items purchased were half a gallon of oil, two vulcanised tubes and a spare clip for the 'Stepney' wheel, indicating a fairly trouble-free journey.

Vincent, during his East Anglian journeys in 1906, suffered hardly any mechanical trouble, but on one venture with Claude Johnson in the Rolls Royce, they succumbed to tyre problems on no less than six occasions.

In general, it seems that minor breakdowns were not uncommon, but motorists would be fairly adept at correcting simple faults, which were accepted as the norm. Let us hope that the experience of one owner of a 3.5hp Benz dogcart was exceptional. A note in the Ipswich registration records for 1906 states, 'never used, was found useless and therefore destroyed'!

The tar gang, Ashbocking, c. 1925. One of the main complaints directed at motor cars related to the clouds of dust they generated in the dry summer months. Although many ideas were tried, it was the tarred surface that finally solved the problem.

CHAPTER THREE

THE INTER-WAR YEARS

After the First World War there was a great demand for motor cars which could not be satisfied, and second-hand vehicles were fetching a premium. This spurred many new firms into production, and by 1919 there were 134 British marques available. During the war, many people had their first direct experience of motorised travel, and subsequently the emphasis changed from owning a vehicle for pleasure and status to the more practical one of personal transport. This need for cheap transport led to a significant increase in the sale of cars, motorcyles and cyclecars, although the latter generally had a poor reputation. However, post-war production problems were only beginning to be resolved when sales were hit by recession and many of the new businesses went into liquidation. The Lowestoft firm of James, Talbot & Davison was badly affected by difficulties in obtaining parts for their new car venture, while the ambitious plans for the Woodbridge-built 'Suffolk Royal' never materialised (see Chapter 6).

The loss of sales spurred several manufacturers into a price-cutting war, with the Morris Cowley being reduced by £180 in 1921 to sell at around £350. By this time William Morris had streamlined the production of his cars along American lines and therefore was better placed to reduce prices than many of his competitors. One firm to benefit from this was Lock & Stagg Ltd of Friars Road in Ipswich, established around 1919. William Morris visited the company and appointed them main distributors and decreed that they should remain so for as long as he lived.

Herbert Austin was also convinced that the public wanted small cheap cars, and the resultant Baby Austin continued in production until 1937, being copied in the process by many other makers.

Prior to the war, most cars were of the open tourer type, offering little protection to the occupants. By the early '20s the power of the engines and braking systems had improved and heavier enclosed bodies began to emerge, although the open car was still the most common type and remained so until the early '30s.

The traditional English weather combined with an open car meant that most non-essential motoring was confined to the summer months. One business motorist, recalling a trip from Ipswich to Fakenham in February 1921, only passed three other cars in a journey lasting nearly four hours.

LOCK & STAGG, Ltd.,
─ AUTOMOBILE ENGINEERS, ─

An up-to-date Garage and Service with modern plant and a skilled
staff who satisfy you by efficient workmanship at fair charges.

MAIN DEALERS FOR MORRIS CARS, HILLMAN CARS,
MORRIS-COMMERCIAL AND THORNYCROFT VEHICLES.

FRIARS ROAD ─────── IPSWICH

TELEPHONE 3155 (2 lines).   TELEGRAMS : MORSERVICE.

*Lock & Stagg were established in 1919. When William Morris came to Ipswich he appointed the
company as main distributors, and decreed they should remain so for as long as he lived.*

In the summer of that same year, not only did more cars appear on the road but
caravanning began to be promoted as the latest form of holiday. The Wingrove Motor
Company of Ipswich were selling caravans in three different sizes: 12, 17 or 22 feet
long. It was claimed that they could be successfully towed by a 10hp car when
carrying four passengers, and could be easily dismantled and stored in a small space.

Advances in steering and suspension were followed by the general introduction of
four-wheeled braking. This brought about such an improvement that a red triangle was
often fitted to the rear of such cars to warn any following motorist of their deadly
stopping powers.

With the renewed enthusiasm for motoring after the war, motor gymkhanas
regained their popularity. They were usually held in the grounds of a large house such
as Hintlesham Hall or Rookery Park, Yoxford. Balancing the car on a see-saw and the
Academy race were two common events, the latter requiring the lady passenger to
draw a picture of an animal, with the prize going to the driver who identified it in the
shortest time.

The increased volume of traffic on the Suffolk roads meant the authorities had to consider means of reducing the inevitable congestion and number of accidents. In 1927 the Ipswich bypass was under construction, and two years later Woodbridge was also to benefit from a bypass, which helped to relieve the chaos at the Cross Corner.

The Autocar referred to the new Harwich–Felixstowe tunnel in the 2 April 1926 edition. It stated that the new tunnel for vehicular traffic, which passes under Harwich Harbour and connects Essex to Suffolk, had been officially opened the previous day!

The old dust problem was now being replaced by one of noise pollution as the volume and speed of traffic steadily increased. One spirited Suffolk lady took action to prevent passing motorists disturbing her husband who lay ill in bed. She appeared in court and was fined £2 for strewing nails and tin-tacks on the road near her house.

Nowadays, we tend to think of the '20s and '30s as a period of peaceful motoring as there were so few vehicles on the roads. There were certainly fewer vehicles, but motorists had none of the present-day advantages such as improved roads, tyres and brakes, together with the increased safety benefits from seat belts, driving tests, drink/drive laws, and so on. The local newspapers of the time gave graphic accounts of the death and carnage that occurred due to motor accidents. These descriptions and the ensuing coroners' reports and court cases filled many columns each week.

Accidents have always occurred on the Ipswich to Norwich road. In one incident at the Stowmarket crossroads, a car swerved, hit a telegraph pole, performed two

Fairhead & Sawyer started their business in early 1920. Their first advertisement read 'E.A. Fairhead and J.C. Sawyer beg to inform the inhabitants of Woodbridge and district that they have recently entered in partnership as Motor and General Engineers at Melton. Mr Fairhead served with Messrs Vickers for four years and Messrs Armstrong Whitworth for two years. Mr Sawyer has been with M.T., RASC for five years and previous to that with a leading firm of Motor Engineers in London.' This photo was taken around 1925 and shows Arthur Fairhead leaning against the pump, with David Girt and Jack Cook to his right. The car is an 8hp Rover.

somersaults and landed on its roof. Fortunately the occupants were not seriously hurt. A motorist on the Woodbridge bypass was not so lucky. While attempting to extricate a wasp which had entered his car, he lost control of the vehicle, which rolled over and killed him.

It is perhaps inevitable that the freedom and pleasure of motoring should also have a dark side. The increased mobility provided by the car was often taken advantage of by those whose livelihood was gained outside the law. In 1929, a headline in the *Suffolk Chronicle* read 'Motor Bandits in Suffolk'. During one raid, safes were removed from premises at Cliff Mansions, Felixstowe; Fairhead & Sawyer's garage at Melton, and a shop in Saxmundham.

Alcohol-related incidents were common, although there were no real objective methods for proving intoxication. A chartered accountant was stopped in Iken by a policeman who saw his car weaving across the road. The man was unable to walk a straight line, and in the ensuing court case it was revealed that he had been convicted twice before for the same offence. This time he was fined £20 and disqualified from driving for ten years.

After the First World War the membership of the Automobile Association continued to grow, and reached a quarter of a million by 1925. The Association was very active in providing road signs as this responsibility did not fall to the local authorities until the 1930s. By 1927 the AA had erected 27,000 village nameplates throughout the country, but these were considered helpful to the enemy in the Second World War and the majority of them were removed, never to be replaced. The Ipswich Transport Museum in Cobham Road has a number of these signs, and is well worth a visit.

W.J. Coe of Ipswich were agents for the Galloway car, and this delightful photo shows Alice Coe behind the wheel of one in 1925. The dickey seat was used in fine weather, but her two sisters squeezed in the front when it rained.

Victor Brewster opened his Sparhawk Street garage in 1920, specialising in repair work and motorcycles. He had an agency for Morgan and New Hudson, but would also obtain and service other cars for his regular customers. This invoice relates to such a purchase from T.H. Nice, one of Bury's early motorists.

Gordon Robinson was recruited into the AA in 1929 through his brother, who was already a patrol man. The main AA centre was at Norwich, and Gordon's first patrol was in the Ipswich area. Initially he was confined to a bicycle for his patrols, and was limited to carrying a few tools, maps and a red flag. His normal duty would be as a relief patrol on one of the main roads, often the London Road between Ipswich and Stratford St Mary, giving assistance to any AA member in difficulty. The new recruits would also spend much time on point duty at the AA boxes that were located on the main roads. Communication with stranded motorists would often be via word of mouth from people who had passed the breakdown.

Gordon's pay amounted to £3 per week, plus 3s (15p) for maintenance of his bicycle, and an extra 10s (50p) for any member he was able to enrol. It was therefore not uncommon for him to earn £5 a week, at a time when most wages were around 30s (£1.50). From Monday to Saturday he was required to work from 9 in the morning till 8 at night, and from 10 till 9 on Sundays, with about every fourth Sunday off. This was for fifty-one weeks a year, with one week's holiday – to be taken in the winter! His first job was to assist a Rolls Royce with a puncture, and he was given a 10s (50p) tip by the owner for providing assistance to his chauffeur.

Relations between the AA and the police were generally good, although they had to be tactful over the question of speed traps. From its very inception, the Association had been at odds with the police because of their warnings over speed traps. The AA patrol man had to salute every member that he passed, and if he failed to do so, this meant there was either a speed trap ahead, or there was a message for that driver, who would then stop and be informed of the situation by the patrol.

After two years on his bicycle, Gordon Robinson received his smart yellow Chater Lea motorcycle and sidecar complete with acetylene lamps. This was eventually replaced when all the patrols were told to report to Thetford Station, where they received their new BSA outfits. The considerable amount of equipment and spare petrol that could be contained within the sidecar meant that these patrols could offer very useful service in the event of a breakdown. There was no official training for the patrolmen in those days, and men would normally be

When Gordon Robinson joined the AA in 1929 he patrolled around the Ipswich area on a bicycle, with tool kit, maps and red flag. He then progressed to this Chater Lea outfit.

taken on if they had a mechanical background, learning the job as they went along. Although breakdowns were frequent, the cars were less complex than today and repairs could often be effected by the roadside.

The AA also published reports in local newspapers stating the condition of the main roads, the location of roadworks, and so on. Even by the late '30s, the presence of horses still needed to be considered, as witnessed by the following letter in the 1936 *Bury Free Press*.

> Sir
>
> May I make my annual appeal to all motorists during the present heatwave, to give way more than usual to our friend the horse. Even an empty van with 'way on' is a trouble to pull up and restart; the few seconds conceded are surely nothing by comparison with the good turn done.
>
> Yours faithfully
>
>
> Steenson Cooke
> Secretary, The Automobile Association

By the mid-1920s, the East Suffolk Police were receiving many complaints regarding the damage to roads caused by buses and lorries with solid tyres, which were still limited to 12mph. There were no official police vehicles at that time, so in April 1924, the Police Authority purchased a 3.5hp Triumph motorcycle combination, with a view to checking the speed of buses and lorries. A 'Bonniksen' speedometer was located in the sidecar, and the aim was to follow the vehicle for half a mile, and to use a stop-watch in connection with the mileometer. In the same year, a speed trap was ordered from Pages of Ipswich. The large box contained a timer and telephone, with a quarter of a mile of cable that would be hidden along the roadside.

The Triumph was not the first official vehicle, as the registration books show 9.5hp Standards registered in 1914 to the East Suffolk Police for public service. Also, the Chief Constable, Superintendents and some Inspectors received an allowance for using their own cars on police business. As early as about 1909, Superintendent John Newson of Beccles received such an allowance for his Anglian car, which was also made in Beccles.

The first driver of the Triumph was Frank Pearl, who had served a four-year apprenticeship with Egertons before deciding to follow in his father's footsteps and join the police force. His previous training made him the ideal person to be involved with the newly acquired machine. At the end of the year, the outfit was replaced by an open two-seater Wolseley 10hp car, with dickey seat. This car was used extensively for speed-testing work, and the occupants always operated in plain clothes. In those days PC Pearl's main job was to check the speed of lorries and buses. The police were not

The first police car to be used for speed testing in East Suffolk was a 10hp Wolseley, seen here at Tuddenham in 1925 with PCs Pearl and Furbank. The main concern at this time was damage to the roads caused by heavy vehicles, which were still retricted to 12mph, whereas the limit for cars was 20mph. Police uniform was not worn for these patrols.

In August 1935 police raided the Butlin's Amusement Park in Felixstowe and removed fifty-three gaming machines, which were alleged to contravene the Gaming Acts. Thirty uniformed police arrived in a furniture van and arrested seventeen people, including staff and customers. From the left, PC Stannard, Inspector Clarke, PC Mummery and Sgt Pearl with the Morris 15–6 used in the raid.

over concerned with car drivers, who enjoyed the higher speed limit of 20mph and caused less damage to the roads. As the Wolseley was the only official vehicle, its drivers had considerable freedom to patrol as they wished along the roads of East Suffolk. After 30,000 miles, the Wolseley engine gave up when a piston saw the light of day through the crankcase.

1930 saw the introduction of the Road Traffic Act, with compulsory third party insurance, the establishment of specific driving offences and the complete abolition of any speed limit. This free-for-all lasted until March 1935, when a 30mph limit was applied to built-up areas only, and remains to this day. An important requirement for the country motorist was to stop after an accident involving the death of an animal. Previously, this clause had only referred to horses, but was now extended to cover cattle, asses, mules, sheep, pigs, goats and dogs. In the discussion stages of the Bill, all manner of animals were proposed, with one MP even suggesting that elephants be included. The elephant problem on our roads has fortunately diminished, but quite how you could kill one in a car without actually stopping is beyond comprehension.

Vehicle registrations were increasing to the point where a new system became necessary. It was originally intended that the numbering would finish at 999, when a further two letters would be issued. For Ipswich, this point was reached in 1913, when they simply carried on with four numbers, until 9999. Additional letters, namely PV, RT and GV were subsequently introduced for Ipswich, East Suffolk and West Suffolk respectively. In later years, these were prefixed with another letter, to keep up with the ever-increasing number of vehicles. (Appendix E provides further details on registration letters.)

Before 1934, you could take to the road without any knowledge of driving or road safety, but in that year the driving test was introduced, with the aim of reducing the growing number of people killed and injured each year.

The extra police involvement with motorists due to the 1930 Road Traffic Act saw the acquisition of cars for patrols in all forces. East Suffolk bought two Morris Oxfords and two Morris Major open tourers, along with four Brough Superior and two BSA sidecar outfits. Vehicles were now stationed at Ipswich, Lowestoft, Eye and Leiston, and the patrols all wore uniform instead of plain clothes.

This powerful 30hp Ford V8 saloon was in use with East Suffolk police by late 1935.

The Oxfords lasted five years and were then replaced by a Morris 15-6 saloon, which was soon handed over to the Halesworth Division. A change of manufacturer in late 1935 saw the arrival of the first of three Ford V8 30hp saloons, which proved to be powerful and comfortable cars. The last police car to be obtained before the outbreak of the Second World War was a Humber Super Snipe 27hp saloon, which was to provide faithful service for a great number of years. Frank Pearl remained with these cars throughout his time at Ipswich, and only left the patrols on his appointment to Inspector in 1948.

It seems inevitable that motorists will come into contact with the law at some time during their motoring career. Changes to the Buttermarket in Ipswich in the mid-1930s were the reason for many such conflicts. It was made into a one-way street, and although the system seemed to work well, after a year or so it reverted to two-way traffic without any official announcement. Needless to say, the ensuing confusion caused a number of accidents and subsequent court cases. To improve safety in Ipswich, in 1935 a scheme was proposed for seventy-one Belisha crossings, at a cost of £765.

Sgt Pearl at the wheel of the Ford V8.

Traffic lights were first introduced to this country in 1928. Many years later, the author recalls that as a young boy on outings to the seaside, at the approach to the Leiston traffic lights (the only set in a wide area) there would be much speculation over their likely colour. These essential aids to safety at major road crossings had been in use at Leiston and Stowmarket since at least 1935, although a local businessman described them as 'a menace to shopping and delivery in Leiston'.

Looking through the *East Anglian Daily Times* for 1930, it soon becomes apparent that many of the facets of today's busy lifestyle are not so new after all.

Frequent complaints were made about 'excessive noise from motor-cycles' and 'the cost of parking, often up to five shillings' (25p).

The Scapa Flow Society, formed in 1893 to check on the abuses of public advertising, published a letter to Shell Mex Ltd, thanking them for their support for protecting the countryside from disfiguring advertisements.

A BP advert for petrol offered £2,000 in cash prizes.

Ford offered free car licences for a period, on either their 14.9 or 24hp models, which were to be sold for the same price.

However, for one man, the motor age seems to have been too much. His private advert stated: 'Exchange 1926 Ford Ton Truck for good working horse, or sell £25.'

To give an indication of the cost of new cars in 1930, the following were being offered in Ipswich.

Egertons	Singer	Luxurious Six	£250
		Economical Junior	£160
	Wolseley	Hornet	£175
		County Saloon Deluxe	£450–695
Lock & Stagg	Hillman	14hp	from £275
	Morris	Minors	from £130
		Cowley	from £162
		Oxford	from £275
		Isis 6	from £375
Popplewell		Austin 7s	£140

Mann Egerton were agents for several makes, and were also able to cater for the client requiring the very highest standards in motoring. There has always been a limited market for more expensive cars, and at that time they were able to offer an ME four-door Weymann Sportsman Saloon on a Daimler 20/70 chassis for £970, or a 6.5-litre Bentley chassis with Weyman coachwork for £2,313. Eighteen Morris Minors could have been bought for the cost of the Bentley, and the ratio for a Metro to a Bentley is still similar today.

The early 1930s were a time of recession, when people were more concerned with being able to run their cars than exchanging them for the latest models. One Botwood's correspondent writing in the company newsletter for 1931 had this to say, 'It may surprise some readers to learn that many farmers who already own cars cannot use them because they are unable to afford the attendant expenses – licences, insurance, running costs, etc. – yet this is definitely true.' The motor trade was to remain depressed for much of the decade.

Although we tend to think of the restoration of old cars as a fairly modern phenomenon, there is a record of a very worthwhile rescue back in 1934. A rare 1899 Panhard et Levassor, which had originally been delivered to the Honourable C.S. Rolls, was sold within a year to a Colonel Mayhew for £1,200, and used in the 1,000-Mile Trial of 1900. By 1901, though, Mr Dawson of Groton near Boxford had bought

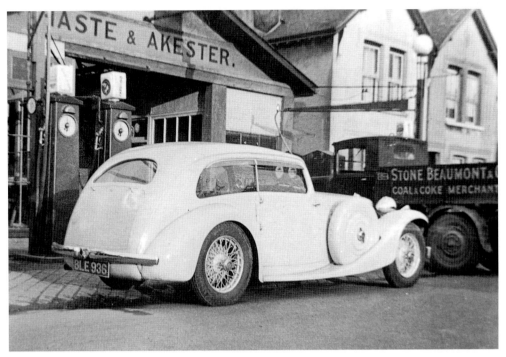

Haste's Garage, Lattice Barn, Ipswich. Archie Haste ran this garage between 1925 and 1935 with his partner George Akester, holding agencies for Hillman and Morris, under Lock & Stagg. The business was sold to Charlie Claxton in 1935, which is the approximate date of this photograph. The car is an SS1 Airline saloon.

it for £650, representing a considerable drop in value in such a short time. For the next thirty-three years it did loyal service on Mr Dawson's estate, with the coachwork finally being replaced by a truck body for the groundsman. In 1934, Miss Dawson presented the car to Colonel Hubert Egerton, and it travelled the 18 miles to Ipswich in fifty-five minutes. Its last journey was to be a trip around Ipswich with Colonel Egerton and two lady passengers in turn-of-the-century motoring costume, prior to being presented to the Museum in Norwich, where it is still on view in the Strangers Hall Museum. Miss Dawson must have been a far-sighted lady, as many of the early cars were left to rot before being broken up.

The *East Anglian Magazine* started publication in 1936, and soon included tips for the motorist and features on new cars. The first one was called 'On Safari in Suffolk with a Vauxhall Fourteen', by Tawstock Courtier. The idea for the article seems to have been a road test combined with a potted history of everywhere en route. This account has been edited to remove the history lesson, but still portrays the general feel of motoring in the '30s.

> Starting from Northgate, Ipswich, at the Mulberry Tree the car is travelling at 25 mph in top gear. Woodbridge Road hills are taken in the car's stride and outside the restricted area we pass the Rushmere Golf Links with the speed indicator needle hovering near 50 and the car behaving just as the advertisement said it would!

R. Watson of Aldeburgh traded as The Eastern Automotive Olympia, of Victoria Road, and placed large adverts in The Autocar, *claiming over one hundred quality second-hand cars in stock. These were often photographed in the town. The seafront shelter behind this 1928 six-cylinder Delage is still there, although the bathing huts have long gone.*

Through Martlesham village and by the Red Lion Inn we find immediate necessity for application of the brakes. By good fortune for the young man riding the bicycle, the car is brought to a standstill almost within its own length, and that after a speed of almost 30mph is reached in seconds.

Woodbridge by-pass road with its fine surface and excellent visibility tempts us to leave Woodbridge town.

Our rear seat passengers have just expressed approval of the Vauxhall's riding comforts. There is a marked absence of road-shocks, a feeling of travel off the surface of the road, 'as though we were gliding along'. Independent front-wheel suspension is responsible for this non-existence of road shock.

Wickham Market is in view. Watch its church spire with a small bell quaintly hung on the outside apparently disappear as we approach.

It's getting hotter. Let's bring this ventilation system into play. No draught ventilation justifies all the claims of its patentees and the system is operated from within the body by drivers or passengers. To those who motor for fresh air and regret the passing popularity of the open touring body, Vauxhall, with its no-draught ventilation offers something that more than makes up for what they imagine is missing.

Morning coffee at Saxmundham and we have time to enjoy the beauty of the Vauxhall as it stands in the roadway outside. There is sufficient streamlining about the car to give it place in the fashion book of 1937 and yet a restraint that has added dignity to the dictates of fashion. 'A thing of beauty . . .' applies to the modern car.

At Yoxford we find that the car's speed has given us time for a detour to Dunwich. From the tops of Dunwich Cliffs we get a sight of Southwold to the north and away to the South, Leiston and Aldeburgh.

At Blythburgh the AA patrol turns us left to Halesworth. This is a second-grade road according to the guide books and the Ministry of Transport, but the Vauxhall continues the journey in just the same way as it has done over roads which are more favourably designated in the guide books. Forty, forty-five, fifty miles an hour and not a tremor!

Through Bungay and onto Scole for lunch, we must ask the Vauxhall to give of its best. The road is good, the car willing and some sixteen miles are covered in 27 minutes, which time has permitted the thorough observance of all road signs and hazards, and the courteous consideration of all other road users.

The old inn at Scole is a place where one finds enjoyment in loitering on the staircase and through its ancient panelled passages. Our journey takes us through Hoxne, Botesdale, Finningham and Cotton before we reach the Ipswich–Norwich turnpike, one of the fastest lengths of road in East Anglia. Watch the speed needle. Thirty-five, forty, fifty, fifty-five, fifty-eight, sixty . . . sixty-two! Exhilarating pace to a driver conscious of a feeling of full control and safety, and happy in the knowledge that his passengers were unconscious of the speed attained.

The gallows sign to the Magpie at Stonham rears across the road marking the ten miles to Ipswich. Still behaving well, the speedometer clocks 100 miles as the Vauxhall comes over the brow of Whitton hill at 55mph.

Tea-time. And at Ipswich again. We have covered 103 miles and have used four gallons of petrol. Twenty-five and three-quarter miles per gallon is good consumption of spirit when it is considered that most of the touring was done within the forty–forty-five range and at times up to sixty!

Convinced now! Don't you think that a Vauxhall will help you to enjoy your touring more? The Vauxhall Saloon De Luxe on either 12 or 14hp chassis – which is optional without extra cost – must be somewhere very near top of the class for value in money.

Hughes Filling Station, Pakefield, c. 1938. The owner of this Hudson Terraplane had the choice of several different brands of fuel and oil.

Today's parking problems would have been impossible to imagine in those days, but in 1937 Bury St Edmunds Council was already debating the question as there was considerable congestion on market day. They decided that if a car park was really necessary then the expense was unlikely to exceed £5,000, and there was a useful piece of land available at the Playfield.

For the motorist, the '30s represented a period when a wide range of reliable cars was available, from the most basic of transport through to sports cars and luxurious saloons. In country areas there was relatively little traffic and no parking restrictions, so a day's outing would have been a pleasant experience.

As many villages had a garage, complete with hand-operated petrol pump, journeys could be undertaken with less concern over running out of fuel. The whole country was now covered by a complex pattern of distribution depots for the petroleum companies, and competition was keen. Noel Cotton joined the Anglo American Oil Company as a vanguard at the Framlingham depot in 1935. It should be remembered that the greatest volume sales were not for petrol, but for lamp and heating oil, with names such as White Rose and Royal Daylight. Much of Noel's time was spent on deliveries to outlying shops and farms. The delivery lorry had a large removable tank as petrol and oil could not be delivered on the same journey, to avoid the risk of filling up with the wrong product. On completion of the oil round, there was the laborious job of changing tanks before a supply of petrol could be taken to a local garage's underground storage tank. Individual customers could still buy the sealed 2-gallon cans.

There is much of interest in this rural garage view. W. Goodwin was a motor, oil and steam engineer, boiler smith, haulage contractor and inspector of machinery. The woman is operating a Bowser petrol pump, while the mechanic, still with hammer in hand, takes a break from the rear axle problem.

Pratts was a well known brand of motor spirit. This aerial view is of their Cliff Quay, Ipswich Depot in 1932. The spirit was marketed by the Anglo American Oil Company, which was the British subsidiary of Standard Oil of America. From 1935 the name was changed to Esso ('S.O.' for Standard Oil).

The declaration of war in September 1939 was to have a dramatic effect on all aspects of life, including private motoring. Noel Cotton was despatched to buy tins of green and brown paint, and set about camouflaging the silver storage tanks at the depot. On 16 September petrol rationing was introduced, with the low-octane 'Pool' petrol being the only type available, at 1s 6d (7.5p) per gallon. The amount you could buy was related to the horsepower rating of your car, and varied between four and ten gallons per month. For essential work 'supplementary' coupons were available. Many people simply decided to lay up their car for the duration, and return to four-legged transport. East Suffolk County Council felt it necessary to issue the following statement.

> Owing to the rationing of motor spirit, it is believed that many residents in East Suffolk are intending to use horse-drawn carriages and the County Council beg to remind such persons that licences must be taken out for these vehicles. The licence duty payable each year is:

Carriage with less than four wheels	15s	(75p)
Carriage with four wheels drawn by one horse	£1 1s	(£1.05)
Carriage with four wheels drawn by two horses	£2 2s	(£2.10)
Hackney carriages	15s	(75p)

In the coastal region there was great concern over the possibility of invasion, and an order was issued in July 1940 that prevented any private car being used on any road within five miles of Lowestoft, Southwold, Aldeburgh, Felixstowe and other east coast towns without a special permit. If a permit could not be obtained, then the car had to be moved outside the zone or immobilised by removing strategic parts and handing them to the police.

Generally, various restrictions and the lack of petrol meant that private motoring virtually ceased, although there were always some people who seemed to have adequate supplies. Vehicles also had to be fitted with blackout hoods on the head-lamps. The author's father-in-law recalled making prototype covers for the Home Office in 1938.

Despite the reduced numbers of vehicles on the road, 1941 is still credited as the worst year for road deaths in Great Britain, with 9,169 people killed. The sharp increase in fatalities at this time was mainly from pedestrians being knocked over, despite a night-time speed limit of 20mph. More Britons were killed by motor cars in the first three months of the war than by hostile action at home or abroad. The roads were mainly used for military and commercial purposes while some cars and lorries towed or carried gas bags on the roof.

It was to be a long time before private motoring fully recovered, and petrol rationing continued until May 1950.

The open road beckons for the driver of this car outside the Bull Hotel in Long Melford. Today the view is little changed, except for the increased volume in traffic.

CHAPTER FOUR

BOTWOODS OF IPSWICH

Botwoods was one of the earliest companies in Suffolk to be involved in motoring, and was also one of the largest, due to its development from an established coach-building firm. Its history can be traced to before the motoring era, when William Botwood moved to Suffolk from his family home in Shropshire. He settled in Ipswich and joined Henry Bennett's coach-building company in Fore Street. As an engineer, Botwood had considerable talent, having invented and patented more improvements in carriages than any other manufacturer.

After the death of Henry Bennett in 1861, the business was carried on by his widow Emma. By 1868 William Botwood had become a partner in the firm of Bennett & Botwood, but by 1875 the partnership was dissolved and William set up in business on his own account. He built a large works on land adjacent to his home, Maple House in Woodbridge Road, to manufacture the finest quality modern carriages. Showrooms were opened at 49 St Matthews Street and were used until new buildings were constructed for the purpose in Carr Street, around 1893. William was unable to take full advantage of his flourishing business and, after two years of poor health, died in 1896.

His first and third sons, William and Samuel, inherited what was probably the foremost coach-building business in East Anglia, and traded under the name W.T. & S.E. Botwood. The working hours of the company were 6–8.30am, 9am–1pm, and 2–6pm, a ten-and-a-half-hour day. Trade apprenticeships lasted five years, and wages were 3s (15p) per week for the first year. The indenture required, among other things, that 'the apprentice was not to contract matrimony nor play at cards or dice or tables or any unlawful game, nor should he haunt taverns or playhouses'. The firm's catalogue offered seventy-five different types of landau, brougham, carriage, cart, gig, shooting wagon, and two types of rickshaw. Apart from the home market, they were exported to America, Australia, Africa, India, China, Japan, Europe and the Colonies.

The construction of a carriage would take up to three months, and involved many people with a wide range of skills. An example of their high standards can be judged from the occasion when a new employee from London admitted to faking a panel that had a crinkle in it. Although not immediately obvious to the eye, Mr Thompson the foreman was so outraged that he threw a hammer through the panel and shouted 'Now fake that!'

55

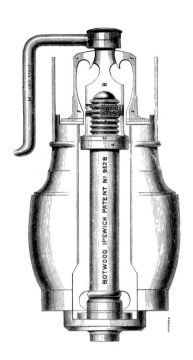

Botwood's had an established reputation as coach builders in Ipswich. Various patents were registered, including this design for a carriage axle hub.

The advent of the horseless carriage was to have a dramatic effect on all coach firms, but Botwoods saw the impending threat and decided to enter the motor trade.

Around 1900, Charles Warren joined the firm, and in December of that year he obtained their first agency – for the French car, Gobron Brillié. Engines and chassis were imported and Botwoods built the bodies for them. These cars were unconventional as their twin-cylinder engines each had two pistons per barrel, operated by separate crankshafts. The pistons moved towards each other to form a central combustion chamber in the barrel. Although extensively advertised, the cars did not sell in great numbers, possibly due to unorthodox design in other areas as well as the engine. This engine could happily run on alcohol fuel, and the 1901 catalogue claimed it would perform equally well on gin, brandy or whisky! In 1904 a 13.5-litre Gobron Brillié became the first car to officially exceed 100mph, when it was timed over a flying kilometre at Ostend.

To expand the motor business, Mr Chapman, who had been a foreign correspondent for Ransomes, Sims & Jefferies Ltd, accompanied Samuel Botwood to Paris to act as an interpreter for negotiations with the De Dion Bouton company. These discussions proved successful and resulted in Botwoods obtaining the agency for these cars.

An important change occurred when Justin Reginald Egerton, or Reggie as he was usually known, joined the business around 1902, and a separate company, Botwood & Egerton, Motor Engineers, was formed. Although the coach-building business continued separately, the move clearly demonstrated that Egerton, like many other pioneers, had foreseen that the motor car was here to stay, at a time when most people

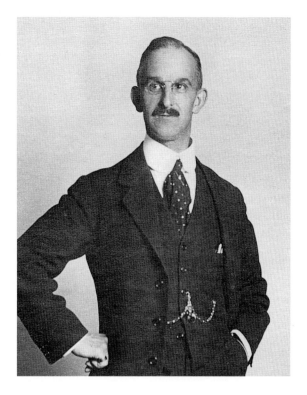

William Botwood. He and his brother Samuel inherited the coach-building business at the beginning of the motoring era, when their father died in 1896.

considered it to be a noisy unsocial beast with no future. In a speech he gave in later life to celebrate the Golden Jubilee of his own company, he remarked how the gathered dignitaries would never have considered the possibility of attending such a luncheon with him in the early days.

> Why not? Because I was the bad boy, actually having the audacity to drive one of those horrid motor vehicles – so dangerous, why they can actually travel faster than a horse can go. They were all against me, as was almost the entire public. So no wonder they would not grace such a gathering as this in my honour – most certainly not!! The only influential concern not against me was the *East Anglian Daily Times*, for which I have always felt very grateful indeed.

Reggie was born in 1873 in Weston Rectory near Norwich, where his father was the rector. At the age of 18 he set off for Canada, and farmed in a remote area of south Saskatchewan for about five years. He recalled that the land could be bought for $3 an acre at the time. In 1897 he left Canada and headed back to England to become involved with the new motor car industry. His brother Hubert Egerton became sales manager of the De Dion Bouton British and Colonial Syndicate Ltd, headed by S.F. Edge, another great pioneering motorist. In 1901, Hubert was introduced to Gerard Mann, an electrical engineer, through a mutual friend, Dr Burton Fanning. Thus the Norwich firm of Mann Egerton was born. It might easily have been a different name, as Hubert had previously approached a number of Norwich coach builders with a view to starting a motor company, but they had seen no future in the automobile. Hubert's early motoring exploits provided the initial experience for this new company, which was to eventually take over Botwoods.

Meanwhile, Reggie was rapidly gaining *his* motoring experience, and in 1900 drove a De Dion motor bicycle to the London Motor Show in Islington. He then took the first Gladiator car onto the show stand prior to the start of the famous 1,000-Mile Trial. The Gladiator was a French car sold under agency by the Motor Vehicle Company, also headed by S.F. Edge. The Trial was intended to allow people to see a car in close up for the first time. Starting in London, the route ran to Bristol, Birmingham, Manchester, Kendal, Carlisle, Edinburgh, Newcastle, Leeds, Sheffield, Nottingham, and back to London. At each main location the cars would be put on show for one or two days. He claimed to have competed in the Trial, although records only refer to his brother Hubert.

Reggie also drove a Century Tandem from Paris to the French Riviera, and worked for Century for a short time. In 1901 he was employed by the Hovis Bread Flour Co and had use of a Decauville for business purposes. This was an early example of the company car, and was possibly his main reason for taking the job.

Always fuelled by enthusiasm, and notorious for his clashes with the law, Reggie was to be the greatest promoter of the motor car in Suffolk. There is unlikely to have been anyone else in the area who could claim to have driven many hundreds of miles over England and the Continent in 1900 and 1901, including night driving.

Woodbridge Road workshops, c. 1905. Originally built for the manufacture of carriages, they readily adapted to the motor car.

CORNER OF MACHINE SHOP

EXTERIOR OF WORKSHOPS. IPSWICH.

The new company of Botwood & Egerton was established in part of the Wood-bridge Road works. Charles Warren's younger brother Herbert joined the firm at this time and, at 15, claimed to be the first motor mechanic apprentice.

Reggie introduced many customers to the company, and orders for several Argyll limousines were obtained. The first landaulette body was fitted to a Siddeley chassis, and the first two-seater body to a 10hp De Dion. Lady Cobbold gave permission for this car to be exhibited at Olympia, where De Dion representatives saw it. They were suitably impressed and asked for quotations to produce bodywork. After much negotiation, Botwood & Egerton received the first order for thirty-six bodies, and the chassis were delivered in crates from France.

Cars and motoring in general were often promoted in the early days by long-distance trials, with John O'Groats to Land's End being the ultimate test. Botwood & Egerton were agents for the German Primus car, and Reggie decided that an endurance run would be the best way to promote it. In January 1903 he and young Herbert Warren attempted this route, but atrocious weather conditions in Scotland forced them to give up and head back to Ipswich. (The pioneering spirit was obviously in the Egerton blood as his brother Hubert was the first person to ride a motorcycle from John O'Groats to Land's End in September 1901.) The following edited account of their epic journey appeared in *The Motor Car Journal* in February 1903.

> Late on a recent Saturday, accompanied by my young mechanic, Herbert Warren, I arrived in Ipswich on my little Primus car after a most eventful journey, and was met in Carr Street by a large cheering crowd. On Thursday, the 15th, at 6.40am, we left John O'Groat's House. It was almost dawn, a bitterly keen wind blew in our faces, ice and snow lay all around as the car sped southward over miles and miles of large, newly-laid-down granite. Wick was not much awake, but, fortunately, there were a few stragglers about who directed us on to the right road. Near Latheron, down went one front tyre. 'That's what we expected, oh, those beastly stones!', but it wasn't the stones at all, the inner tube had been badly pinched under a clip. This was the sole and only tyre trouble we had of any sort, despite the fact that 'we carried weight' in the shape of spare things, and thirty gallons of petrol, etc. We came to Berriedale long before we expected, but scenting danger we crawled down to find that it really was the famous Berriedale Hill; and it was well we did, for the turn at the bottom is so dreadfully sharp that at any ordinary speed it would be impossible to negotiate it. After climbing the long, steep ascent on the other side, we took a wrong turn and did not discover our mistake till we had gone eight miles inland.
>
> At Inverness the road leaves the coast, and one is soon in the heart of the Highlands. The moon was now up and we could see pretty clearly the white track before us, but on going up one or two steep hills, we found the snow deeper and deeper, till there was not more than a faint wheel track in a boundless expanse of snow. Slower and slower became our progress and deeper and deeper got the snow, till at last we thought we must be on some disused track and hopelessly lost. It was impossible to turn the car round owing to the great depth of the snow on each side, so we kept crawling forward. 'Crawling' for that is the best word, as for some time the high gear had had to be abandoned for the second, and at

59

last the first had to be resorted to. We plodded on till at last we were actually climbing down fairly steep hills on the low gear, and then at the rise the engine wouldn't do it. What was to be done? We tried driving on the low gear and shoving at the same time; but one cannot do much of that, and realised we were stuck. Near at hand was a cottage to which in time, we walked and rapped upon the door. Soon a head looked out, 'Puir bodies, have ye been in the snow all night? We won't be long and will let you in.' While the good woman dressed we sat down on the snow, and were immediately asleep. 'You'll catch your deaths sleeping in the snow,' in a kind Scottish voice came upon my sleepy brain, as I awoke. In the afternoon, with four men pushing hard, we managed to get the car out of the drift, and turned round on the way back to Inverness.

'Ugh!!!' 'Are you hurt?' 'What bad luck; now our trip is all over.' 'Railway gates; why don't they light them?' With a terrific shock the car had suddenly been brought to a standstill! We had collided with an iron railway gate, unlighted, right across the road! I went in search of the station-master, and said a few words. The wonderful thing is that he quite agreed with me and said he always had considered those gates were dangerous as they were never lit up. We three then inspected the damage with lanterns, and looked and tested, nothing broken and nothing bent could we find except a slight leak here and there. But the iron gate, though double-strutted on both sides for strength, was hopelessly upset, and the top rail, was broken in two, and the whole gate was bent and doubled in the middle.

After passing through Keith the snow again got deeper, till at length each slight climb was all we could manage. Now coming to a fork road, with a sign post which pointed to places unheard of by us, we feared taking the wrong one. Therefore, espying a farm some way off the road, we left Miss Primus to look after herself. We tapped gently at the door for some time, and got an answer at last. When we got back we found the cracked radiator leaking like a sieve. The petrol pipe also was leaking fast. This I managed to put right by making a new flange to the copper pipe. We pushed the car back down the hill, it was very hard work, and at last got it to the bottom, where was another farm. The inmates by this time, were having breakfast, and we very readily joined them, after which we took off the leaky radiator, and proceeded to mend it with rubber tape and solution. It wasn't a good mend, but it certainly stopped it from leaking quite so fast, and as soon as possible we got on our way again. They told us, however, that we must return to Keith, as the road by Huntley was not opened yet. We did not reach Turriff without great loss of time, for the leaky radiator burst out afresh, and we plugged up the waterholes with corks and pieces of iron to keep them in, and ran on only one layer. The engine got very hot indeed, but no lubrication troubles occurred. At Turriff we put up at the Commercial Hotel, had a very good dinner and actually went to bed. This was Saturday night, and the first bed since leaving John O'Groat's early on Thursday. We did not get away till after noon on Sunday. With my poncho on over my motor coat, I was proof against all weather. The 'Sabbath' is not the best day to get things in Scotland, so we were lucky in being told of the Caledonian Motor Company, where we found the manager, most obliging. Soon we were on our way south, and stayed the night at the Commercial Hotel, Stonehaven. On Monday morning we journeyed south

Reggie Egerton and Herbert Warren boarding the Primus outside the John O'Groats Hotel, January 1903. The atrocious weather conditions in Scotland forced them to abandon the planned route to Land's End and they finally reached Ipswich ten days later. The extra 30-gallon tank behind the headlamp reduced the time spent looking for places to buy petrol en route.

through Montrose and Arbroath, soon reaching the Marmalade town. Here we had great difficulty in finding the ferry from Dundee to Tayport, and were charged 4s 10d to cross. After passing over the most appalling roads to Fifeshire, which had had much more snow than some of the parts we had just come through, we arrived at 2.30pm at Balfour. It was Wednesday noon before we were able to get away, and 3.15pm before we could cross the ferry from Burntisland to Granton. We took the road through Edinburgh, Haddington, Dunbar, and Berwick as, having once departed from the old historical route to Land's End, I had decided to run down to Ipswich.

The roads now were very bad; a good deal of snow had fallen, which had thawed and frozen, and partly thawed again. When within a few miles of Morpeth we went down a short, steep hill, and partly up; but when on the steepest part the car, with hind wheels going forward, began to slide backwards. The hill was one sheet of ice covered with a little water. We tried everything we knew to get up that hill, but having no rope or anything to wind round the tyres to give them a grip, we failed entirely.

On Friday we journeyed through Darlington, Northallerton, and Thirsk, and here I could not help noticing the splendid way in which the roads were made, and what skill, care and attention must have been given them. On the Saturday we drove through Newark, Grantham, and Peterborough and then over abominable roads to March, Ely and Newmarket. Then to Bury, and over perhaps the worst bit of the lot, to Ipswich. The distance is roughly, I believe, about 870 miles in all, and we traversed every kind of road in every kind of condition, experiencing every sort of weather, except thunder. We were about six and a half days running – a good test for the Primus.

In this account, he omitted one particular incident when Herbert was looking for a petrol leak with a match! Fortunately, the ensuing fire was put out by a hostler who doused it with a few buckets of water.

Over sixty years later, Reggie reflected how the car had really been very poor, with many bad points, such as belt drive, no clutch, side chains, and unequal size wheels. He sold it to Mr Swinburn at Snape Priory, and reckoned it led a charmed life as he considered the new owner 'treated the poor thing most shamefully – not on purpose but because he had no mechanical instincts whatsoever'. Mr Swinburn was unfortunate enough to roll the car over on the Wherstead Road and the Primus had to be towed back to the garage for repairs. The public must have shared Reggie's true feelings for the Primus as only three had been registered in Ipswich by the end of 1904.

Through his motoring exploits he gained great experience, and was looked upon as a knowledgeable, outspoken promoter of the motor car. The report on a 1903 Club run to Saxmundham refers to him twice: as a 'good samaritan of the party' for mending someone's puncture, and as a 'mechanical genius' for starting another person's car.

In 1904 Reggie attracted the attention of the police by driving in a manner dangerous to the public, in Princes Street, and was convicted by the Ipswich Magistrates. He subsequently appealed and went to considerable trouble to provide objective evidence to support his case. Along with William Burton of Burton, Son & Sanders, he carried out experiments to determine how long it would take to stop the car, as much had been made of this aspect. From the claimed speed of 17mph, it was established that it could stop in twice its length, and from 10mph within its own length. The respondent in the case said 'This is a sort of reconstitution of the crime, the sort of thing they do in France.' However, it must have impressed the Recorder as he quashed the conviction. The incident was widely reported in the motoring press as it was claimed to be the first successful appeal against the new Motor Car Act. By this time J.R. Egerton's name would have been well known to people interested in motoring, and his case would have gained useful publicity for the company. Looking back on those pioneering days, he had this to say in a speech he made in 1960.

> Motoring in those early days was most certainly not all fun, and for the slightest thing one would probably be summoned, especially someone like me, and so I have been summoned for every conceivable thing. Even for a horse running away in a field some distance from the road on which I was driving, and for having a tail lamp, the red of which had faded to orange, but it was no laughing matter to me then, and I was always convicted. I was convicted by Ipswich Magistrates of dangerous driving because a dog ran out and got run over, so I had to appeal, the very first appeal case under the Act. I won the appeal.

In fact, he was rather muddled up with his convictions, which is quite understandable considering the number.

In the first decade of the century Egerton had many brushes with the law regarding motoring offences. This early summons for exceeding the 12mph limit was received when he was living at Northwich, before his move to Ipswich.

The following is a synopsis of some of Reggie's early brushes with the law:

June 1902	West Yorkshire. Summons for speed in excess of 12mph.
March 1903	Summons for driving at a rate of more than 12mph. He was taking a JP to Ipswich station when a dog was run over. Despite conflicting evidence, and the presence of a Magistrate in his car at this time, the Bench found the case proved and fined him £2.
March 1904	Convicted of speeding in Princes Street. Subsequently made first successful appeal under new Motor Car Act.
August 1904	Charged with 'driving a motor car at a speed dangerous to the public' down Copdock Hill. This case came before the Samford Bench, where Charles Berners, a pioneer motorist, was in the chair. Case dismissed.
December 1904	Fined £1 for not keeping lamp burning to show registration plates.
April 1905	A police sergeant declared his speed down Woodbridge Road as 'dangerous', despite being 400 feet away from him.

He was not stopped at the time, and had no idea of the offence until he received the summons. Consequently there were several witnesses against him, but none for him. Mr Vulliamy, his solicitor and a keen motorist, said that the case would never have come before the Bench if it had been anyone but Mr Egerton. The majority of the Bench found the case proved and he was fined £5.

June 1905   Speed dangerous to public, across Cornhill. Again, he was not aware of any offence until he received the summons five days later. Convicted and fined £5.

August 1905   Speed dangerous to public at Barrack Corner, 11.10pm. He was notified of the offence seven days later, and was now fearful of losing his licence. In order to find witnesses, he placed an appeal in the newspapers. When the case came before the magistrates they considered that much of the evidence was conflicting and gave him the benefit of the doubt. Although the costs were high, the Eastern Counties Automobile Club voted against assisting him. But the members and friends of the Club started a subscription and raised £31 18s 6d (£31.93) for him.

February 1906   Collision with bicycle at the station, and summonsed for driving at a dangerous speed. The Bench were divided on the matter and did not convict. They were, however, 'unanimously of the opinion that Mr Egerton should use more caution in driving through the town'.

In most of these cases, Reggie was driving his 8hp De Dion Bouton, registration DX11. When he decided to sell the car, in November 1905, it was advertised as 'The famous DX11', and he offered a 100-mile trial run to any genuine buyer.

Throughout the country, police were active in their enforcement of speed limits, but it does seem that he was singled out for special attention. A photo caption of him in *The Motor* in 1905 refers to 'Mr Egerton of Ipswich, who has been the object of persistent irritation by the police in the town'.

The policeman on the beat now had considerable powers over the upper echelons of motoring society as he could apprehend without warrant. It was not even necessary to stop the driver, provided he was notified in writing within twenty-one days and there was more than one witness. This time delay usually precluded the defendant from finding any witnesses in his own defence. After two convictions for exceeding the speed limit, a court could then suspend a driver's licence on a subsequent offence. The original court case descriptions highlight much contradictory evidence, where the public witnesses had no real point of reference to judge the speed of vehicles. The Botwood family must have had very mixed feelings about their new business partner, who regularly appeared in the local courtrooms. Reggie probably felt there was no such thing as bad publicity.

Reggie Egerton and his 8hp De Dion Bouton, which was well known to the local police force. When offered for sale in 1905, it was advertised as 'the famous DX11', with a 100-mile trial run to any genuine buyer.

Botwood & Egerton took on apprentices to learn the motor trade and, in 1905, in their first year they were paid 5s (25p) a week. These apprenticeships lasted five years, and the wage would increase by 1s (5p) a week each year. Although the hours were limited to a maximum of fifty-eight per week, they were required to work on Bank holidays. They were also entitled to a fortnight's annual holiday. By 1906 a new apprentice had to supply his own tools, as Reggie claimed it would 'make him, when a man, worth more to himself and to his employer than if he had not been in the habit of looking after his own tools'. The firm offered to supply the tools, with a 10 per cent discount if paid in cash. It was clear by this time that the motor car was here to stay, and many young men decided there was a worthwhile future with it.

Other young men just enjoyed driving cars, and Lord Brougham's son, who was at school in Felixstowe, ran up bills of £70 with Botwood & Egerton for the hire of cars and motorcycles. In the ensuing court case to recover the money, Lord Brougham said it was disgraceful that tradesmen should encourage schoolchildren in such extravagance. He won the case and the firm lost their £70.

The continued expansion of the company saw additional agencies being added, and in 1906 they included De Dion Bouton, Argyll, Gladiator, Darracq, Siddeley, Wolseley and Humber. There is no mention of the Gobron Brillié that had been so actively promoted only a short time before, and the Primus was no longer manufactured. The company presented a Challenge Cup for reliability trials, which was won in 1906 by A.J. Snowden in a 16hp Argyll.

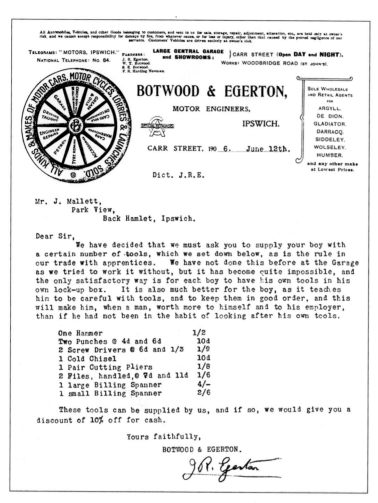

All Automobiles, Vehicles, and other Goods belonging to customers, and sent to us for sale, storage, repair, adjustment, alteration, etc., are held only at owner's risk, and we cannot accept responsibility for damage by fire, from whatever cause, or for loss or injury, other than that caused by the proved negligence of our servants. Customers' Vehicles are driven entirely at owner's risk.

TELEGRAMS: "MOTORS, IPSWICH."
NATIONAL TELEPHONE: No. 84.

PARTNERS:
J. R. Egerton.
W. T. Botwood.
B. E. Botwood.
F. R. Harding Newman.

LARGE CENTRAL GARAGE and SHOWROOMS: } CARR STREET (Open DAY and NIGHT).
WORKS: WOODBRIDGE ROAD (ST. JOHN'S).

BOTWOOD & EGERTON,

MOTOR ENGINEERS,

IPSWICH.

CARR STREET, 190 6. June 12th.

Dict. J.R.E.

SOLE WHOLESALE AND RETAIL AGENTS
FOR
ARGYLL.
DE DION.
GLADIATOR.
DARRACQ.
SIDDELEY.
WOLSELEY.
HUMBER.
and any other make at Lowest Prices.

Mr. J. Mallett,
    Park View,
        Back Hamlet, Ipswich.

Dear Sir,
    We have decided that we must ask you to supply your boy with a certain number of tools, which we set down below, as is the rule in our trade with apprentices. We have not done this before at the Garage as we tried to work it without, but it has become quite impossible, and the only satisfactory way is for each boy to have his own tools in his own lock-up box. It is also much better for the boy, as it teaches him to be careful with tools, and to keep them in good order, and this will make him, when a man, worth more to himself and to his employer, than if he had not been in the habit of looking after his own tools.

One Hammer	1/2
Two Punches @ 4d and 6d	10d
2 Screw Drivers @ 6d and 1/3	1/9
1 Cold Chisel	10d
1 Pair Cutting Pliers	1/8
2 Files, handled,@ 7d and 11d	1/6
1 large Billing Spanner	4/-
1 small Billing Spanner	2/6

These tools can be supplied by us, and if so, we would give you a discount of 10% off for cash.

Yours faithfully,
BOTWOOD & EGERTON.

When the partnership dissolved in 1910, William Mallett was still an apprentice and it was unclear where he would transfer his allegiance. He was offered an extra 2s (10p) per week by the Botwoods, combined with a reduction in hours from 58 to 54. Egerton offered improved working conditions, claiming that his new Northgate works were heated by hot water and lit by electricity, and that a healthier workshop did not exist in Suffolk. Mallett chose to remain with Botwoods.

Mr Herbert Birkett joined Botwood & Egerton in 1908 to take charge of the workshops – another example of how the company was able to attract experienced personnel at a time when few such people existed. Previously, Birkett had worked for both the Lanchester and Wolseley car companies, and had been responsible for taking the first Wolseley to Russia, where he established an agency for them.

In the same year, Enoch Akester joined the company, when the Carr Street premises were run by two brothers, E.P. and H.F. Groves. H.F. was required to provide a night service for customers who needed assistance or a tow-in. Enoch was to take over the night duty after Reggie had a heated exchange of words with H.F., who duly resigned.

As official repairers to the Automobile Club of Great Britain and Ireland, the company held all the latest machinery and tools at their Woodbridge Road premises, where all types of work were carried out, including the manufacture of bodies and vulcanising. There was also an upholstery department where cape cart hoods, leather hoods and motor driving aprons were made, as well as the normal upholstery. In 1906 over 100 complete motor bodies were manufactured at the works. The foreman lived opposite and was available to customers 'in distress' when the works were closed.

Motor cars were not the only line of business at this time; the company also sold motor boats and had one for hire which could take fifteen people.

Contracts were obtained in 1908 to produce twenty-five bodies at a time for Napier. (Reggie probably knew S.F. Edge, the original driving force in the production of Napier cars, through their earlier involvement with the Gladiator.) Napier chassis were carted from Derby Road Station and the yard would often be full of them as it took a long time to complete each car. Early car manufacturers invariably produced the engine and chassis only, with the owner having the bodywork of his choice supplied by a local coach-builder. The Napier was a well made car, but expensive. In 1906 the cost of the bare chassis varied between £650 and £1,500 for the four models on offer.

A branch of Botwood & Egerton was opened in the High Street, Newmarket, where they were keen to attract the custom of the horse-racing fraternity. To this end, a ladies' sitting room was provided, furnished with tables, chairs, sofas and mirrors. There was also a covered wash-down yard, large enough to hold several cars. This was important as chauffeurs were usually required to wash and clean their cars at the end of each day, no matter how late they arrived or how bad the weather. Mr Burrell the manager, lived

Herbert Birkett, another pioneering motorist, came to work for Botwood & Egerton in 1908. He had previously taken the first Wolseley to Russia and had established an agency there. This photograph is remarkable for the car he is driving. It is the Renault racing car in which Marcel Renault was killed during the 1903 Paris to Madrid race. It was subseqently rebuilt and sold in Britain.

on the premises, with his foreman and two mechanics. Needless to say, there was always someone available after normal working hours.

In 1910, there was a strong disagreement within the company and Reggie resigned his directorship. On starting his new company, Egertons (Ipswich) Ltd, he received a telegram saying 'Prosperity to Egerton, freed from bondage', which suggests that matters had not been running too smoothly for some time. He opened new premises in Northgate Street, which some people considered were far too large, yet the company continued to expand. The Crown Street premises were built in 1928, and eventually extended over 100,000 square feet. Several car agencies were held, with exciting long-forgotten names such as Angus-Sanderson, Arrol-Johnston, Belsize Bradshaw, Ruston Hornsby, and Talbot-Darracq, as well as AC, Dodge, Lagonda, and Wolseley.

Of all the people encountered in the research for this book, Reggie Egerton emerges as the most dynamic character, unafraid to speak his mind, or write numerous letters to newspapers furthering the cause of motoring and his business. No doubt he did more to put the car on the map in Suffolk than anyone else in those formative years. He was intensely interested in all mechanical matters: he gave lectures on the internal combustion engine and was involved with the newly formed Aeroplane Club in 1909. It seems inevitable that such an outspoken personality would eventually go his own way. The impression is gained that although Botwoods could see the future of the motor car, their hearts were still with the carriage trade.

A parallel situation occurred with Reggie's brother Hubert, who left Mann Egerton & Co Ltd in Norwich around the same time. From correspondence in later life Hubert

A branch of Botwood & Egerton was opened in Newmarket to attract the custom of the horse-racing fraternity. It was sold in 1910 when the partnership was dissolved. Customers were well looked after, even to the provision of a ladies' waiting room.

made it quite clear that he had provided the impetus for the expansion into motoring, as Gerard Mann was an electrical engineer with no experience of motor cars.

The firm of Botwood & Egerton was dissolved, and Botwoods Ltd was formed in August 1910 to take over its business and that of W.T. & S.E. Botwood, the coach builders. Major Arthur Whatman, an underwriter, purchased £4,000 of ordinary shares to become a director at an annual salary of £200. The Newmarket business was sold and a number of agreements signed with car and component suppliers, including:

> Michelin Tyre Co, Vacuum Oil Co, Dunlop Pneumatic Tyre Co, Rover Co, Ford Motor Co, Humber Co, Standard Motor Co, Avon India Rubber Co, Anglo American Oil Co, Palmer Tyre Co, Mogul Tyre Co, Deasy Motor Manufacturing Co, Sunbeam Motor Car Co, De Dion Bouton, The London and Parisian Motor Co, Napier, and Willys Overland.

A company brochure was produced which made passing reference to horse-drawn carriages still being available, but this was by then a dying trade. If customers had taken them up on the following offer, they would certainly have accumulated a considerable amount of secondhand horse-drawn equipment.

> To patrons who are desirous of using motor cars in lieu of horse-drawn vehicles, Botwoods offer exceptional facilities for doing so on the best terms as, owing to their extensive carriage business, they are able to purchase from such patrons the horse-drawn vehicles, harness or complete turn outs they desire to dispose of, at better prices than could be obtained elsewhere; and, owing to the motor car business, Botwoods are in a position to offer any car at the lowest market price.

They regularly had a stand at the Motor Show, where the Carr Street garage attendant was instructed to keep the cars polished and remove finger marks left by prospective purchasers. Strict limits were set down for the expenses of directors and employees, as follows:

Directors: Bed and breakfast 7s 6d (37.5p), lunch 2s 6d (12.5p), dinner 3s 6d (17.5p)

Employees: Bed and breakfast 3s 6d (17.5p), dinner 1s 3d (6.25p,) tea 9d (3.75p)

Negotiations were opened with Mann Egerton & Co Ltd in 1912 with regard to a take-over of the shares by that company, but the matter was subsequently dropped. Two years later, William Botwood resigned his directorship and left the company. By the time of the First World War, the production of coaches and carriages had fallen considerably, and soon ceased altogether as the firm concentrated hard on the motor trade. Mr W.D. Chitty joined the company in 1915, and became sales manager before leaving in 1919 to form his own business, W.D. Chitty Ltd, the Ford Dealers in Diss, Norfolk.

The agencies held by any company would vary depending on the viability of the manufacturers. In the years leading up to the war, Delage, Briscoe and Scripps-Booth were added to Botwood's already extensive list.

The Sunbeam car was enjoying popularity at that time, due in part to their success in motor racing. When E.C. Ransome, the mayor of Ipswich, ordered a six-cylinder model from Botwoods, Enoch Akester was despatched to Wolverhampton to collect it. At the factory he was handed a telegram stating that Mr Ransome was staying in Cambridge and was to be collected on the return journey. Enoch duly picked up his passenger, hoping that he would not want to drive. But the inevitable request came, and young Enoch was hardly in a position to refuse. All went well until they came to a bend in the road approaching Newmarket. The car went wide, took to the grass and crossed a drain, collapsing a back wheel. The Sunbeam then swerved across the road and overturned. Enoch was very seriously injured, with both jaws fractured and extensive damage to the base of his skull. The *Suffolk Chronicle* report stated: 'Mr Akester, whose condition was first supposed to be hopeless, had some chance of recovery.' Mr Ransome suffered severe shock, and his teeth supposedly fell out later!

There is a further twist to this tale as there was a third party in the back of the car, who probably thought his luck could not get any worse. Mr Craven had lost his right leg in a motorcycle accident a few weeks earlier and had been to Birmingham to have an artificial one fitted. Taking advantage of a lift back to Ipswich, he was lucky to be spared further serious injury.

The outbreak of the First World War had a disastrous effect on many of the businesses that were reliant on private motoring. Botwoods were fortunate in obtaining

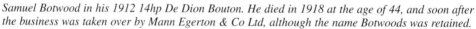

Samuel Botwood in his 1912 14hp De Dion Bouton. He died in 1918 at the age of 44, and soon after the business was taken over by Mann Egerton & Co Ltd, although the name Botwoods was retained.

Government contracts for the production of commercial vehicle bodies, and in late 1914 an urgent order was received for eighteen ammunition trucks. But there were staff shortages as so many had joined the Army, and Mr Turner was sent out to try and find men for the work. For this particular job a number of Overland touring cars were used, with the bodies removed so they could be converted into trucks. Work carried on for several days and nights until they were completed, when they were collected by a company of the Suffolk Regiment.

In 1916, the Government proposed to take over the Woodbridge Road works, but the directors argued that they were providing an important service by maintaining the vehicles used by public servants. They eventually won their case and alternative premises were found for Government purposes.

Towards the end of the war, the company was kept busy looking after the needs of farmers, and was actively promoting the Wallis Junior farm tractor.

A Mann Egerton take-over was again being considered in 1918, mainly due to the efforts of Sir Arthur Churchman, but Samuel Botwood had become very ill and, despite a long vacation, died in November of that year at the age of 44. His death was a great loss to the company as he had been a very popular and well respected employer. A year later Mann Egerton took over the majority of the shares to become the holding company. The old name was retained, and they traded as 'Botwoods Ltd, Associated with Mann Egerton & Co Ltd'. But by this time there was no longer an Egerton in the company for Hubert had left around 1910.

Gerard Mann took a very keen interest in his new company and visited Ipswich once a week, always trying to better his time for the journey from Norwich. He soon got to know the staff at Botwoods and would make a point of asking anyone's name if he did not already know it. The new parent company was from the next county though, so they were rather looked upon as 'foreigners'.

By the early 1920s the production of any car bodywork was rare indeed, but there was one hangover from the old coach days – the firm still received rickshaw wheels from China for retyring.

The increased popularity of motoring after the war created a need for larger premises, and in 1923 a site at the end of Carr Street was purchased, which necessitated the demolition of Majors House. Charlie Minter was serving his apprenticeship with the company at this time and one of his jobs was to help the farming clients who came to the market each week. Prior to the building work they had been allowed to park their cars – many of them Model T Fords – on the Majors House site. A particular problem with the T in cold weather was the drag caused by the oil between the clutch plates. On starting, this could result in the car taking off down the road by itself. To overcome this, the standard practice was to jack up one of the rear wheels and then start the engine, which caused the raised wheel to turn. With the foot pedal in the middle neutral position, the brake would then be applied and this freed the transmission. The owners would often give Charlie a tip for his service and, with some twenty cars, it was a good bonus. There seems to have been considerable variety in his apprenticeship, as another duty was to act as temporary chauffeur to Sir Arthur

The first showroom was on the north side of Carr Street. This photo was taken some time between 1919, the year of the Mann Egerton take-over, and 1924, when larger premises were opened at Majors Corner. Note the tramlines in the road, which caused problems for cars pulling up at the garage. When Egerton started his own business in Northgate Street he advertised the fact that there were no tramlines outside his premises.

Churchman, driving him in his Rolls Royce to the Portman Road factory. Sir Arthur did not smoke – he considered it bad for his health – but gave Charlie a voucher that could be exchanged at his factory for 200 cigarettes.

The new buildings at Majors Corner were completed in 1924 and incorporated showrooms, offices and a garage, but within about three years the adjoining site was purchased and further buildings constructed for the repair and service departments. The centralisation of the company meant that the old Woodbridge Road Works could be sold, and this severed the final link with the old coach-building days.

The late '20s and '30s were difficult times for most companies, and Botwoods were no exception. Their main agency was by now Austin, which was heavily promoted by events such as 'Austin Week', when the cars were paraded through the streets of Ipswich. The local authorities co-operated in this exercise by putting the traffic lights out of action so the procession could proceed smoothly.

Another highlight of the '30s was the Austin film show in the Regent Theatre. Some 12,000 invitations were sent out and a loudspeaker van toured the streets. This ensured large crowds at the cinema, but could not guarantee to have a similar effect on sales. During this period there were many references to 'weathering the storm' and 'pursuing new business and consolidating goodwill'. To this end, the staff were all provided with new uniforms. The showrooms were also equipped with lighting at night, although the famous neon lights did not make their appearance until 1937.

In addition to Austin, the main agencies at this time were BSA, Citroen, Daimler, Humber, Lanchester, Rolls Royce, Rover, SS, Sunbeam, Standard and Talbot. And for

The new showrooms at Majors Corner provided plenty of natural light to show off the cars. The sporting trophies belonged to Major Whatman, a director of the company. These 1927/28 models are, from the left, Austin 10hp tourer, 12/18hp Minerva saloon, Fiat Tipo 509A saloon, Austin 7hp and Rover 9/20hp tourer.

The first-floor coachwork department at Majors Corner in the late 1920s. Extensive accident repair work was carried out here on the timber framework of cars, under the watchful eye of Bill Turner. Note machinery powered by the large electric motor bolted to the floor, with some belts partially guarded.

A carefully posed photo of the spray shop. Note the absence of any masking materials.

something completely different, there were departments selling lawnmowers, wire-lesses, and 'Li Lo' pneumatic mattresses. The female staff of Botwoods had a distinct advantage over those who worked elsewhere as they appeared to be able to afford several different pairs of shoes. This impression was achieved by taking their shoes to the paint department, where they would be resprayed to a new colour.

Trade began to pick up in 1934, when the company was able to declare its best year since 1927. Their slogan for 1934 was 'Buy Bigger Cars' as it was thought that Suffolk people who could afford a larger car were not doing so, being small-car minded. The psychological approach to car sales was a subject much discussed and written about within the company, ever anxious not to miss an opportunity to replace a client's old banger with something more modern and in keeping with that person's position. It must have been a bit of a struggle, though, as Suffolk people are often reluctant to spend money to part with something that has served them well for many years.

By the mid-1930s, Botwoods were certainly able to offer large cars, including the following American models:

Buick 8 Viceroy Saloon	£465
Chrysler Kew Airglide Six	£345
Chrysler Croydon Airflow Six	£510

(During the same period, Egertons were selling the Packard Six.) These prices can be compared with those of the Austin range offered by Botwoods in August 1935:

Seven Saloon	£112 and £120
Ten Saloon	£158 and £172
Light Twelve Four Saloon	£198 and £216
Heavy Twelve Four Saloon de Luxe	£295
Sixteen Saloon	£318
Eighteen hp York Saloon	£328

Although the luxurious American cars were very desirable, they did not find as many purchasers as the cheaper established products of the home market.

Business had certainly improved by the end of 1936, and there were now delays in obtaining new cars as the manufacturers' order books were full. But it was not long before the threat of war was again hanging over Europe. However, the Company News Bulletin of June 1939 was optimistic:

> It seems a possibility that we may escape war, and that a period of comparative prosperity may supervene. Should this prove to be the case, let us, one and all, make the most of our opportunities.

The optimism was soon replaced by preparations for war. Large quantities of black paint were applied to the rooflights of the building and white lines were painted around the edge of cars to increase their visibility at night. If that was not enough to keep the paint shop busy, foreman Bill Stannard was also chief plane spotter. When the air raid warning sounded, he would rush to his corrugated-iron lookout shed on the roof of the Regent Theatre in order to alert the staff when enemy aircraft were visible.

This small-scale Humber Snipe was on display in the showroom at Majors Corner, c. 1936. It was promoting 'Evenkeel Comfort Seating for Absence of Shock and Pitching'.

The sign attached to the car reads 'One day's collection of Flying Standards, Botwoods Limited'. They were collected from the factory and then driven in convoy around the county, gaining useful publicity. The Abbeygate in Bury St Edmunds is the backdrop here, c. 1937.

Botwoods were not alone in feeling the loss of trade provided by the private motorist, but were fortunate in that they were able to obtain enough commercial and government business to see them through the war years.

Night view of the Botwoods showroom during Talbot week in 1937.

CHAPTER FIVE

A.G. POTTER OF FRAMLINGHAM

Many of the early motor businesses evolved from existing companies, often those trading in cycles. The firm of A.G. Potter in Framlingham was perhaps quite typical. Arthur George Potter, or A.G. as he was usually known, was one of five children, whose parents lived in Needham Market. He served his apprenticeship as a blacksmith, and for a hobby raced 'penny farthing' bicycles. In 1897 he married Rose Pendle from Rendham and, a year later, set up business in Framlingham as a basket maker. Acquiring the sole agency for 'Swift' cycles in the area was perhaps a natural progression, but there was another motive. Walter Fairweather was already selling cycles in the town and had decided to expand into baskets and cane work. A.G. was not happy about this encroachment on his basket business and decided that he too would sell bicycles.

The bicycle had far more importance then than it does today: it enabled people to travel considerable distances for work when previously the only alternative had been to walk – the ownership and stabling of a horse having always been expensive. The early days of the business were a struggle, and A.G. would often have to hire out bicycles to help pay the 4s (20p) per week rent on his property. But by 1901, he had moved to Tomb House, a cycle shop had been built, and he had acquired the use of the old Reading Room as workshops.

His first car was a Rochet with tiller steering, which he bought second hand in 1907 when it was already several years old. The registration slip states that it was a dark blue three-seater, with yellow undercarriage and white wheels. This was followed by a Rover and a Vulcan, which were used for hire purposes. Money to expand into this area was borrowed from Mr Allen, a schoolmaster from Rendham.

The motor business, however, proved even more competitive than bicycles. Charles Garrard had an established ironmongery and engineering business in Framlingham and had opened the town's first garage around 1900. (It is interesting to note that he is not listed in Kelly's directory with any motoring connection until 1912, whereas he had definitely been selling and hiring cars for many years before then.) Although Garrard's larger business enabled him to buy new cars and A.G. was only able to deal in second-hand models, there was some rivalry between the two firms. For both, though, motor-related activities would have been a side line to their main business.

A.G. Potter (1873–1942) started in business as a basket maker, and progressed through bicycles to the sale of Ford cars.

By 1905, Charles Garrard was an agent for the British-built Napier and the French Gladiator, both handled by S.F. Edge's Motor Power Company in London. In 1907–8, agencies for Ford and Argyll followed. At that time the Argyll was probably seen as a more popular car than the Ford, and before long some of Garrard's advertisements made no reference to Ford, although he was still the local agent. (Bear in mind that Ford did not start their subsidiary in this country until 1909.) However, by 1915 the Model T was a bestseller and Garrard was proudly proclaiming himself 'Agent for the famous Ford Cars'.

A.G.'s cycle trade continued to increase, and in 1907 he took on a keen 13-year-old named Morgan Watts to help in that department. When he left school, Morgan's one aim had been to work for a business dealing with the increasingly popular motor cars, and motorcycles and bicycles which were his great interest. The previous year, C.D. Castell had opened a motor garage in Wickham Market and was an agent for the Talbot Car company. Morgan had hopes of working there but his pal Bert Howell got the job as his application was in first. Fortunately, through his brother Percy, a baker in Framlingham, Morgan heard there was a job going with Mr A.G. Potter. He went for an interview and was accepted on a month's probation, becoming the first person on the payroll. Every day Morgan cycled from his home in Wickham Market, arriving at 8 in the morning and leaving at 7 in the evening. The business at that time was primarily related to basketware and cycles, the latter being Morgan's main preoccupation. In fact he had as little to do with the basket side as possible, and would only help with cane chair work in winter when cycle repairs were in short supply. There were also men who travelled around the countryside who would be taken on for a week's basketwork in order to earn enough money for bread, cheese and beer before moving on to another town.

In late Victorian times there had been many improvements in cycling, and the 'ordinary', or 'penny farthing' as it is commonly called, was superseded by the conventional safety cycle. There was a 'penny farthing' at A.G.'s shop in those days, but kept only as a novelty. Morgan remembered riding it, with the attendant problems of trying to get up enough speed before mounting, and the legs bending when turning the 42-inch diameter wheel. Landing in the ditch was not an uncommon experience.

The safety cycles were all fitted with pneumatic tyres by this time, which gave a fairly comfortable ride on the roads, which were not well maintained. However, Morgan well remembered reversing the trend and fitting solid tyres. One of the masters at Framlingham College regularly had the valves removed from his inner tubes. Despite buying a dozen valves at a time, they kept on disappearing, and in desperation he asked Morgan if he could fit some solid tyres. This he did, with the consequence that he had a very uncomfortable ride, and all the spokes came loose!

A.G. held agencies for several different bicycles over the years. The Raleigh and Swift were particularly good makes, the latter being advertised as 'the best in the world'. Many companies in the Midlands were dedicated to the production of cycle parts, and in this way it was possible to build up your own make of bicycle. A.G. sold his own model, calling it the 'Fram'. It was a good sales aid as the name and a transfer with 'A.G. Potter' were clearly visible on each one. His advertisement of the time read: 'replating, enamelling, and repairs of all kinds carefully, expeditiously and cheaply executed'. The replating and enamelling were actually sent to Kenyon & Trott in Ipswich. Mr Trott was keen to drum up business and would arrive by train, complete with bicycle, looking more like a gamekeeper with his moustache and deerstalker hat. He would visit businesses in the town and then cycle on to Debenham and elsewhere to continue his sales tour.

The bicycles ordered from the manufacturers were all well made, and arrived at Framlingham station in crates containing three machines. They were not cheap, though, and prices started at around 10 guineas (£10.50) in 1910. As farm labourers were earning around 10s (50p) a week then, the cycles were very expensive compared with their relative

Charles Garrard held the first Ford agency in Framlingham.. This view of Garrard's Market Hill frontage shows various motoring signs – Pratts Motor Spirit, Vacuum Oils, Napier Motors, Argyll and Motor Union.

A. G. POTTER,

STATION ROAD, FRAMLINGHAM.

And at NEEDHAM MARKET.

Linen, Stable and Arm Baskets.   Skeps, Sieves, and Fancy Baskets.
Chairs Re-seated with Cane.   Taps, Measures, and Wood Goods of every description.

CYCLES!   CYCLES!   CYCLES!

The SWIFT CYCLES are the best in the world.   Prices from £10 10s. 0d.

Sole Agent for the District.

"The Wulfruna" (well-known locally) or any other make of Cycle supplied.

Prices from £6 10s. 0d

Accessories, Tyres, Covers, Etc.,

At Lowest Prices.

Re-plating, Enamelling, and repairs of all kinds carefully, expeditiously and cheaply executed.

Personal Attention Given.

Note Address—

A. G. POTTER, Station Road, FRAMLINGHAM.

The move from baskets to bicycles is evident in this advertisement of 1903.

cost today, and many were sold on 'easy terms'. Meanwhile, Morgan was getting a little tired of cycling to and from Wickham Market every day and, as soon as he reached the legal age of 14, he progressed to a motorcycle.

A.G. Potter acquired his first Ford car in 1909. Records show that in the April of that year, Charles Garrard sold a Model N Ford – with three bucket seats, wooden wheels and extensive brass fittings – to the Reverend Henwood of Badingham for £92 10s (£92.50). (The Model T had only recently been introduced and was still in short supply.) The Reverend was unable to keep the car due to financial problems and A.G. bought it from him, marking the start of a long association with Ford. On many occasions, Morgan would be called upon to drive the local College masters to a cricket match at Easton in this Model N, with two or three on the running boards as well as two in the bucket seats.

When he was only 16, Morgan decided that although working on old cars was fine, he would very much like to drive a brand new one. At about this time, those who could afford it were beginning to feel that a car was essential. The problem was that most people had no mechanical knowledge, which was essential if you intended to drive yourself. The solution was a chauffeur. Morgan had been driving the hire car for Alfred Preston the auctioneer, who lived at Worlingworth. When Preston decided that he needed his own car, Morgan was recommended for the job of chauffeur. He somehow felt it would not last very long, but was keen to try this opportunity.

The new car was a most impressive Siddeley Deasy, purchased from Duff Morgan & Vermont in Norwich. It had a Renault-style dashboard-mounted radiator, wire wheels, and cost around £900. The coach-built body came complete with side screens and a hood with straps that fixed to the front mudguards. A uniform was bought for Morgan, including a white coat and summer hat.

His new job took him to live at Grove Cottage, Worlingworth. These lodgings he considered, were the very best he ever had in his life. With good food and lodgings, 10s (50p) per week wages, and the opportunity to drive a new car, what more could a young lad ask for? It was not that easy, though, as Mr Preston was not too keen on spending money to maintain his new acquisition. However, he did agree to have the barn lined out so the car was less likely to freeze in winter. Maintaining the car certainly kept Morgan busy: as well as the more obvious cleaning duties he had to jack up the wheels to remove flints from the tyres and then fill the holes with solution using a hot iron, and pay regular attention to the multitude of grease nipples. Mr Preston's farm hands often badgered Morgan to help them in the fields, but he made it very clear where his duty lay, and it certainly wasn't in a field.

Every Tuesday he would drive Mr Preston to Ipswich Market, when he would be given half a crown (12.5p) to buy his own lunch. The reduction of this sum to 1s 6d (7.5p) and the general waiting around soon led Morgan to believe that perhaps chauffeuring was not the job for him. Nevertheless, he was no doubt a good chauffeur as Dr Jeafferson in Framlingham had also tried to recruit him. The doctor, who was the first person in the town to have a car, owned an old Argyll with a single-cylinder De Dion engine, which he later changed for a 10/12hp Swift. He saw Morgan on the

A.G., with son Horry, displays a bicycle outside his stand at the Framlingham Horse Show, c. 1905.

Market Hill one day in his smart uniform, and said 'You silly little bugger, why did you not come and work for me?' But by this time, after nearly a year of chauffeuring, Morgan called it a day and returned to work for A.G.

In 1910 A.G. and Captain E.P. Clarke visited the Bournemouth Air Show. There, they witnessed the fatal crash of the Honourable C.S. Rolls, whose name would forever be linked with the most prestigious of cars. A.G. decided that aviation was not for the family man.

The business grew slowly as there was little finance available. The first cars were bought second hand, usually from auctions in London as there were few available locally. Typical examples were an 8hp De Dion Bouton and a Gladiator. Morgan was involved with the refurbishment of these cars as well as looking after the cycle trade and trying to ignore the basket side of the business. He had fond memories of one of the early machines, a three-wheeled AC Sociable that was used as a general runabout. It had a 5hp single-cylinder air-cooled engine and tiller steering. Going round corners was quite exciting as the tiller could be passed to the passenger beside you. These tricycles were capable of nearly 40mph, with a fuel consumption approaching 50mpg.

The expansion of the business required extra staff, and in 1912 Robert Hawes joined the company to officially learn the business of cycle and motor agent, as laid down in his Articles of Agreement. These stated that in return for a payment of £20 from Hawes, A.G.Potter would take him into his employment for six months and pay him a salary of 10s (50p) a week.

A.G.'s first employee was 13-year-old Morgan Watts. After a while he was tempted by the lure of a large new car and became chauffeur to Alfred Preston, a local auctioneer. Morgan drove this Siddeley Deasy for him, but soon became disillusioned and eventually returned to work for A.G. Potter.

The AC Sociable, with family gathering c. 1908. Rear left, Gee Williams, Morgan Watts, A.G. Potter, his wife Rose, and Shumpty Thorpe. Their children are in front: from the left, Horry, Phyllis, Don and Jack. The tyres of the three-wheeler are covered to protect them from the sun.

In about 1910, the Vulcan hire car was involved in an accident. A farmer from Brundish regularly came to Framlingham by horse and trap, leaving them at the Station Hotel so he could catch the train to Ipswich on market day. The return journey usually followed an extended stay in the Hotel bar. On this occasion he was proceeding home, but on the wrong side of the road. The Vulcan appeared around a corner with 'Shumpty' Thorpe at the wheel, and the inevitable happened. Fortunately nobody was hurt, although the car was damaged. Morgan was summonsed to drive the farmer home, as he had done several times before. There was never any charge for this, but A.G. often attended shooting parties at the farm, where all guests were well looked after. The farmer's drinking habits didn't change – the bay mare knew the way home well, even if her well-oiled owner didn't. When the horse died, its replacement was not so experienced, and the trap turned over in Dennington one night. Some locals righted the trap, replaced its driver, and sent them on their way again. On a subsequent occasion when the horse was stopped by Sergeant Scott, the driver fell into the bottom of the cart. He was fined 2s 6d (12.5p), plus costs, for being drunk.

A.G. had been impressed by the suitability of his Ford to the local road conditions and, after negotiations with the company, obtained a sub-dealership under Charles Garrard in October 1913. His first contract enabled him to sell three cars a year. For him this was a substantial commitment, and a considerable change of pace from his basket-making beginnings.

His 1915 Agreement (for twenty cars) set out 253 requirements, including:

The trade area to be limited to the town of Framlingham, and a two-mile radius from the railway station.

A £30 deposit to be paid, which could be forfeited if he did not buy his agreed number of cars.

A garage, showroom, and repair shop were required.

He was to advertise the cars in the local papers, and spend not less than 1 per cent of the retail price of each car purchased.

A Model T standard touring car had to be kept in stock for the sole purpose of demonstration and exhibition.

A 15 per cent discount to be given on the cars.

Elsewhere in the county, the following firms also held agencies for Ford cars.

Ipswich	Egerton's
Bury St Edmunds	S.J. Jenkins
Clare	J. Deeks & Sons
Elmswell	P.W. Hitchcock
Needham Market	D. Kerridge
Sudbury	B.H. Purr
Melton	Page & Girling
Wickham Market	C.D. Castell
Saxmundham	Smith & Wesby
Wrentham	S.G. Sawyer

Vulcan car crash, c. 1910. Shumpty Thorpe was at the wheel of A.G.'s hire car when he turned into Station Road to be confronted by a drunken farmer in a horse and trap, on the wrong side of the road. Fortunately no one was hurt (a broken windscreen was very dangerous in the days before safety glass). A large crowd has gathered and A.G. is standing to the right, hands on hips, surveying the damage.

OPEN and CLOSED CARS
FOR HIRE.

NEW and SECOND-HAND
CARS BOUGHT and SOLD
ON COMMISSION.

THE MOTOR TRADE ASSOCIATION

AUTHORISED
FORD DEALER

CYCLE, MOTOR and TRACTOR
REPAIRS by EXPERIENCED
WORKMEN.
SPARE PARTS STOCKED.

A. G. POTTER, STATION ROAD, FRAMLINGHAM, SUFFOLK.

CAR INSURANCE

CUSTOMERS' OWN CARS
DRIVEN AND STORED AT THEIR
RISK ONLY.

TELEPHONE:

TELEGRAMS:
"POTTER, FRAMLINGHAM."

FORDSON TRACTORS.

Letterhead incorporating the famous Model T.

Ford started their subsidiary in this country in 1909, although the cars had been available for some time before then. Four hundred cars were sold in 1910, and many of the agencies were set up during this period. A year later, a large site was developed in Trafford Park on the outskirts of Manchester, and the Model T was produced there in ever increasing numbers. Henry Ford's ambition had been to build only one model of car, and this he achieved with the Model T.

> I will build a motor car for the great multitude. It will be large enough for the family but small enough for the individual to run and care for. It will be constructed of the best materials, by the best men to be hired, after the simplest designs that modern engineering can devise. But it will be so low in price that no man making a good salary will be unable to own one – and enjoy with his family the blessing of hours of pleasure in God's great open spaces.

The T stayed in production from 1908 to 1927, with over 15 million sold. The early models in this country were all assembled from imported parts, but by 1914 the moving assembly line had arrived. This technique, coupled with the increasing use of British-made parts, enabled prices to be cut further and further.

The Model T had a 2.9-litre four-cylinder engine, which was rated at 20hp. The transmission consisted of a two-speed gearbox with reverse epicyclic gears, operated by foot pedals. Although the car looked rather frail, it seemed to cope well enough with the poor road conditions.

In no time at all this car had outshone all its rivals – mainly because it was well engineered and cheap and therefore offered the best value for money. Over the years, many different body styles became available.

A sub-dealership with Ford was beneficial for A.G. as it enabled him to sell popular cars, with the necessary spares and technical backup that such a large company could provide. The car showroom was in an old building down Station Road, well separated from his cycle shop at Tomb House, where he sold Bradbury and Calcott motorcycles.

Meanwhile, war clouds were gathering, and in 1914 hostilities with Germany had commenced. All aspects of the trade went flat very quickly and although A.G. had a contract for six Ford cars that year, they were not all delivered.

Morgan, who in 1913 had married Hetty Self, decided that, like most of his friends, he would do his bit for King and Country. For him, any involvement with the military would have to have had some connection with cars or motorcycles to make it more attractive. He had seen an advertisement for despatch riders, which seemed to fit the bill, but you needed your own machine. A.G., being the Bradbury agent, agreed that Morgan could have one if accepted for duty. He duly went to Ipswich to sign up, but there was already an enormous waiting list. It was not until January 1915 that Morgan and his pals Bob Hawes and Walter Godbold were asked to report to Cambridge to be examined for duties in connection with mechanical transport. When repairs to the last car had been completed, they delivered it to Bury St Edmunds and then continued on to Cambridge.

Army life was going to be very different from working in a small rural workshop, but there would be compensations, such as 6s (30p) a day.

They departed from Cambridge by train for Grove Park, an old workhouse near Bromley in Kent. The next day they received orders to go to Woolwich Arsenal. The nearby London General Omnibus garage, which had only recently been built, had been taken over and was to be their workshop. For someone like Morgan who was interested in all things mechanical, this was a fascinating place, with steam engines, cars, three-wheelers and motorcycles. He was to spend the next eighteen months there.

In late 1916 Morgan received his orders for France. After a first-stage camp about a mile outside Southampton, he eventually embarked on a heavily overloaded ship that was constantly under threat of attack by submarines. They were led by a destroyer and safely reached Le Havre, but were kept on board for a long time. This was most unpleasant due to the overcrowding, sickness and insanitary conditions.

Morgan was rated as a 'first class' driver in the Army Service Corps, and was sent to Rouen, where the drivers were selected for the lines. From there he was posted on to Albert, which he remembers as being knee-deep in mud. A fortnight passed here, under canvas, as the officer in charge was keen to keep the new driver and lorry for deliveries of equipment to the front lines.

His duties were then transferred to the 88th Anti-Aircraft Battery, which gave support to the 4th Australian Division on the Somme. The transport consisted of a Model T van and two anti-aircraft lorries. Morgan and the other drivers would leave at about 3 o'clock in the morning to reach the forward lines in the open countryside. They were usually the first in position and the last to leave.

The anti-aircraft gun was in its infancy then, as were the aircraft themselves. The first lorries were Thornycrofts, which had been converted at Woolwich by strengthening and fitting slide-out jacks to take the gun recoil.

In the cold winter months, there was a danger of frost damage to the engines. To prevent this, methylated spirits were added to the water and, in addition, a small amount of this mixture would be drawn off and put in a tray. A junior ASC man would then be detailed to watch this for any signs of freezing, in which case the engine would be started.

As part of his duties, Morgan had to do an hour's plane spotting, but recollected that they were very lucky indeed if an aircraft was hit. An artillery gun was used, with an 18-pound charge set off by a time fuse. First, range finders determined the distance, then the gun was aimed. Three charges would normally be fired before corrections were taken, but by this time the plane had usually decided to change course.

A pal of Morgan's was another driver, Jack O'Hara. One day Jack was delivering ammunition to one of the batteries, with his lorry sliding all over the place as the road was made up of boarded sleepers. Unbeknown to Jack, another battery of 18 pounders was partly hidden behind a bank next to the road. As he levelled with them a salvo was fired over the lorry, the blast completely ripping off all the tarpaulins. This scared Jack so much that he managed to stay with the rest of the drivers on the anti-aircraft guns, thus avoiding any further deliveries.

One sunny morning, a German plane started a machine gun attack before they could take any retaliatory action. Everyone took cover below the lorries, and the plane flew off. The artillery officer in charge should have reported the incident as once a location was known, further attacks usually followed. However, the men proceeded to have breakfast – dried bacon cooked on a paraffin stove, which smelt and tasted horrible. Suddenly, the air was filled with explosions as the Germans sent over their 'coal boxes'. These devices exploded in the air, producing lots of black dust, thereby enabling their range to be determined. Morgan sensed this was connected with the

The early business was centred around his cycle shop in Station Road. These Model Ts were manufactured before 1916 – the radiator style was changed that year to a more streamline shape. A.G. is seated in the front car, with his sons behind, c. 1914.

A.G. on a farm visit with his daughter Phyllis. During the First World War he was appointed as a tractor supervisor, with command of various types, including American-made Moguls and Titans.

earlier aircraft attack, and within a few seconds explosive shells were falling all around them. They were in a confined area and could not drive away as the lorry in front would not start. It was always the second driver's job to start the engine, and the jacks had to be removed as well as the blocks from the wheels. Another shell exploded next to his lorry. Part of it went through the bonnet hitting the second driver, severing his arm, and blowing part of his chest away. He was taken to the nearest dressing station, but was already dead. His name was Jack O'Hara. The lorry was washed down to remove the blood, and then driven back to take up position again. The anti-aircraft guns with their crew of seven to eight men were always on the move and as they were in the forward positions were at considerable risk.

After the Armistice was signed, the Army Service Corps was moved to the Rhine to prepare lorries for the massive transportation of men and equipment. Morgan ended up near the anti-aircraft workshops and managed to transfer there, where he worked on the Four Wheel Drive lorries.

In January 1919 he returned home to his family. After landing at Dover, he reached London by midnight and stayed in a Salvation Army Hostel. Early the next day, Morgan walked to Liverpool Street Station and caught the 'paper train' to Framling-ham. He was one of the fortunate ones to return. The town's War Memorial records the names of sixty-eight who did not make it back.

Morgan was keen to return to work, but was not yet discharged from the army, which was to present certain difficulties. A.G. had recently lost his close friend and foreman 'Shumpty' Thorpe, who died of influenza, so he took Morgan to the labour exchange in Ipswich to have him endorsed as the replacement for agricultural work. He had to return to Woolwich Arsenal for his release papers, but on arrival found long queues of soldiers with the same intention. His earlier eighteen-month training period there was not forgotten, and before long he had managed to get through in front of all the others. From there, he was sent to a dispersal camp in Thetford, where he was reprimanded for leaving all his equipment, including his rifle, in France. He returned to Framlingham and was beginning to pick up the threads of civilian life again, when Superintendent Mann knocked on his door, announcing that he had a warrant for Morgan's arrest as he should be in France. The two knew each other well, and the Superintendent was in a quandary over what to do for the best. Morgan realised it was a mistake, but played along with the dilemma for some time before producing his papers, which officially gave him one month's discharge providing hostilities did not recommence. Morgan never did get involved with the agricultural work, but instead organised the cycle trade, which had a large backlog of repair work due to the shortage of spares and labour.

The heavy losses of both shipping and men during the war meant there was an urgent need to increase food production. Resources were distributed throughout the country by the County War Agricultural Committees, and in 1915 A.G. was appointed as a tractor supervisor. He had command of twenty-four tractors of various types, including American-made Moguls and Titans. Prototype Ford tractors were not tested in this country until 1917 and, even then, large-scale production was not able to go ahead immediately as the Government needed the resources to build aircraft, following recent bombing raids on British cities. Production of the Fordson was therefore started in the American Dearborn factory. By the end of 1917 only 254 had been built, but this rapidly increased to 34,167 in 1918.

The situation with regard to food production remained serious, and in March 1918 A.G. held a supper with musical accompaniment for all tractor operators in the area.

Tractor operators were urged to 'plough or perish'! Horry is at the wheel of this American Parrett tractor, with A.G. on the far left and Don kneeling behind his sister Phyllis.

A.G. assessing the likelihood of his Ford traversing the flood in Albert Place.

Mr Tomlinson from Egerton's explained that the position was desperate, and it was a matter of 'plough or perish'.

The Fordson had been the 'chosen' tractor of the Government, and much argument ensued when it was announced after the war that they would be sold off. This represented a change in Government policy as the original intention had been to retain ownership. Production did eventually start at a large purpose-built factory in Cork, and tractors were made there from July 1919. The first Fordson sold by A.G. was to Mr J. Hall of Chediston, and it remained in use until 1955. In 1918 A.G signed a contract to become a sub-dealer for Fordson tractors, under Mann Egerton of Norwich.

Apart from the first year of the war when car production was disrupted, A.G.'s quota was twenty, although the purchasers were less likely to have been private individuals. By 1919 the number had increased to twenty-five, peaking at forty in the following year. He was still only a sub-dealer, though, and Charles Garrard carried the advertisements for Ford in the local press. In November 1920, however, A.G. proudly proclaimed that he was the authorised Ford dealer, with the following new prices:

Touring car (electric starter and lights)	£240.00
Delivery van	£225.00
Ton truck	£210.00
Fordson tractor	£260.00

After this date, Garrard no longer mentioned Fords, but concentrated on first the Overland and then Morris cars.

Leonard Wardley was taken on the payroll in 1920, and was to remain at Potter's for all his working life. He initially worked under Morgan in the cycle shop at 2s 6d (12.5p) per week, but was soon involved with the repair and servicing of cars. In those days, new vehicles had to be collected from the manufacturers, and Leonard would be driven to Ipswich station with £3 in his pocket to catch a train to Trafford Park. If the Model T was ready after lunch, he would travel back to Framlingham the same day. If, as often happened, there were delays at the factory, he would not get away till much later and would have to stay overnight at Rugeley, in a large communal boarding house. When a tractor was ordered, this could be brought back on a one-ton truck.

Leonard remembered the Model T Ford as a very basic reliable car with no frills – and that one of the worst servicing jobs on it was relining the transmission bands.

By the early 1920s Potter's business was growing, and his three sons, Arthur, Don and Jack, were also working for him. An agency for Ransomes Sims & Jefferies was gained in 1920, and this led to contract ploughing for local farmers. After the war, trade took a long time to revive, and A.G. was always keen to be involved with any

ESTIMATE & SHIPPING SPECIFICATIONS
For Year Ending December 31, 1922.

Ford Motor Company,
(ENGLAND) LIMITED
TRAFFORD PARK, MANCHESTER.

In accordance with the provisions of Sales Agreement executed with your Company, for the sale of its products, We/I estimate We/I shall sell at retail the following automobiles, trucks, chassis and tractors for the year ending Dec. 31, 1922, specifying the months in which shipments are to be made without any further or confirming orders, permitting you, however, to change the model specifications or shipping dates to conform to your production as manufactured.

We/I agree to receive, accept and pay for such products in accordance with terms of Sales Agreement.

TYPE	Jan.	Feb.	Mar.	April	May	June	July	Aug.	Sept.	Oct.	Nov.	Dec.	Total
Tour.	1	1	1	1	1	1	1	1	1	1	1	1	12
Run.		1				1		1					3
Sed.		1		1				1		1		1	5
Cpé				1			1						2
Van.	1	1		1	1	1		1			1	1	8
Ch.		1								1			2
T.T.Ch.	1	1		1				1		1		1	6
T.T.		1		1			1	1		1			5
T.V.	1			1		1		1			1		5
Totals	4	4	4	4	4	4	4	4	4	4	4	4	48
Cum.Total													
Tractors	1		1			1		1	1		1		6
Cum.Total													

The hand-written note on this estimate of A.G.'s Model T requirements states that he need not take all (or any) sedans, coupés or two-seaters. By the late '20s, the tractor business had expanded considerably and A.G. Potter was in third place for overall tractor sales in the whole of the country.

This was signed on Tuesday Feby 14/22 on the distinct understanding that I need not take all or any Sedan Coupés or two-seaters

Total Cars for Year   48
„ Tractors for year   6

Dealer's Signature   *A G Potter*

Town   Framlingham

Dated   March 14 19 22

A G Potter
unknown

91

form of work that would ensure continued wages for his men. The firm also sold and repaired wireless sets.

Even in a small market town like Framlingham, competition to gain the custom of motorists was always present. Leonard Walne had already gained much practical experience at Rolls Royce, Armstrong Siddeley, the Lindsay Motor Company, Lock & Stagg, and Egertons, before he set up his own garage in Bridge Street after the First World War.

In 1921 A.G. bought St John's Motor Works in Woodbridge for his son Arthur Horace, known by everyone as 'Horry', and the company traded initially as Potter & Bensley. When Horry wanted to expand the workshops he managed to buy a large wooden army building that was surplus to requirements in Felixstowe. As there was no lorry available, Leonard Wardley and some colleagues dismantled the building and brought it to Woodbridge on a timber drag hauled by two horses.

On another occasion, Horry wanted to have a bungalow built, and took advantage of some buildings being sold off on Orfordness. Leonard was despatched with his friends to demolish the concrete-block buildings. These blocks were taken to the waterside by miniature railway and loaded onto a barge, which took them to sea and then up the river Deben to Woodbridge. After some initial difficulty with the local customs officer, the blocks were delivered and the bungalow eventually constructed by a local builder. Back in Framlingham, another non-motoring job was to take the town's first piped water supply to new bungalows in Saxmundham Road, with water being gravity fed from a tank in the Pump House.

The general increase in demand for cars immediately after the war was not sustained, and manufacturers had to make severe price cuts in order to stay in business. A.G.'s advertisement on 26 May 1923 proclaimed:

Ford makes the most momentous announcement in British motoring	
Lowest prices in history	
Touring car	£110.00
Delivery van	£110.00
Ton truck	£140.00

These were incredible reductions, with the touring car now selling at 46 per cent of its 1920 price.

On the other hand, the tractor business was developing, and Leonard Wardley was asked if he would like to help. One of his first jobs was to carry out repairs, but as there was no transport available, he had to fix his spanners to his bicycle and pedal off to the outlying farms. He soon became disenchanted with all this cycling and bought a belt-driven Triumph motorcycle with a box sidecar, in which his dog Rover travelled.

Further useful business that came from the tractor side was a contract for the groundworks for the new Ipswich airport. With the assistance of Mr Woodrow's steam engines from Parham, A.G.'s men pulled up the oak trees, flattened the hedges and

It is possible that this photograph and invitation relate to the same event. The Model Ts on display here would have been well suited to traversing farm tracks. A.G. is sitting on the Fordson tractor.

A. G. POTTER, Framlingham, in conjunction with Messrs. POTTER & BENSLEY, Woodbridge, are giving (by kind permission of J. LARTER, Esq.)

A Practical Ploughing Demonstration

WITH

" THE FORDSON TRACTOR "

And two different Types of Ploughs

AT COOPER'S FARM, NORTH GREEN, PARHAM

ON THURSDAY NEXT, Aug. 27th, 1925. 11 a.m. to 5 p.m.

You and Your Farmer Friends are CORDIALLY INVITED to this Demonstration. &&&&&& &&&&&& Light Refreshments

---

filled the ditches. The grass was sown and cut just in time for the official opening by the Prince of Wales in June 1930.

By the time production ceased in August 1927, the Model T was considerably outdated and its replacement, the Model A, was eagerly awaited. The following figures show how overall Model T sales in the UK had been falling.

1924	27,449
1925	22,238
1926	21,815
1927	12,520

At the same time, the combined Austin and Morris sales reached 100,000.

A.G.'s order book for Model T cars (including vans and chassis) mirrored the national trend. The estimate for 1920–21 was sixty, but fell to forty for 1925, and sixteen for 1927. The car was available in several forms, as in the following estimate of A.G.'s purchasing requirements, with the open tourer still being most popular.

Estimate of Ford Vehicles for Year 1925

Touring car	15	Ton truck chassis	8
Two-seater	2	Ton truck complete	7
Tudor saloon	5	Ton van	5
Fordor saloon	3	Total trucks	20
Coupé	3		
Van	10	Fordson tractors	6
Chassis	2		
Total	40		

Two years later, the figures show a different picture.

	1925	1927
Model T cars	40	16
Trucks	20	24
Tractors	6	15

Even in a quiet country area where the rugged, simple qualities of the T were respected, its limitations, coupled with the prospect of a new model, meant a falling order book. The tractor side was particularly important at this time, because the new Model A car was not yet available and the T was no longer being produced. This caused difficulties for many dealers, and several changed to alternative makes in order to satisfy customers and keep in business.

A.G.'s optimistic advertisement, placed in December 1927, read as follows:

> To the Motoring and Prospective Motoring Public. Once again, Mr Henry Ford has taken the lead in the car world. The startling new model is being exhibited at Holland Park, London, from December 2nd–10th. A.G. Potter, who is the local authorised Ford dealer, extends a cordial invitation (to all who are interested) to accompany a party visiting the show on Tuesday December 6th, for which he is providing special facilities.

> Touring car, 14.9hp engine £150.00
> 30 cwt lorry   £210.00

His customers were to have a long wait, as only about 5,000 of the new Model A had been produced by the end of 1928.

Bicycles were still an important part of A.G.'s trade, and the numbers sold increased steadily under the watchful eye of Morgan Watts, the foreman. The firm's advertisements for the late 1920s referred mainly to tractor and bicycle sales.

The business was formed into a limited company in 1928. But by the early 1930s agriculture was in a depression, with land prices of only £4 10s (£4.50) per acre, and this had a serious effect on trade as many of A.G.'s customers were farmers. However, in 1930, he took the opportunity to purchase premises on the Market Hill. At that time, the front doors opened to reveal beautiful gardens containing flowerbeds, greenhouses and mulberry trees, but unfortunately these all had to go to make way for the workshops. The Ipswich firm of Cocksedge provided the steelwork at very low cost as they had little work, and it was erected by A.G.'s men.

Apart from business interests, he was very much involved with local affairs, being on the town council, a magistrate, school governor and special constable, and playing the double bass in chapel.

Although the Model A was a good car, Ford considered it necessary to introduce the AF Model, which had a 2-litre 14.9hp engine compared with the normal 3.2-litre 24hp engine. This was to reduce the effect of the tax introduced in 1920, which was levied at £1 per horsepower and replaced the petrol tax. The old Ts with their 20hp engines also suffered in this respect. With the depressed economic climate, people were becoming more interested in smaller cars, such as the Austin Seven, whose purchase and running costs were lower. Ford did not have such a car to offer until 1932, when its first 8hp model was displayed at the Albert Hall. The elegant Model Y with its 933cc engine became the production version of this show car, selling at £120 for the two-door model.

The new car sold well, with sales of 27,000 in 1934, but with increasing competition from cars such as the Morris 8, the price was lowered. In 1935, it was sold as the Popular and claimed to be the first fully equipped car for £100! This cost-cutting exercise was made possible by improved efficiency in the firm's purchasing policy with suppliers. At the same time a larger 1172cc engine was used in the new 10hp Model C, although the body and chassis were different. These were to be the first true European Fords, as the previous ones had been designed for the American market.

The Model A Ford was the long-awaited replacement for the Model T. This 1931 advertisement is from the programme of the historical pageant held in Framlingham castle.

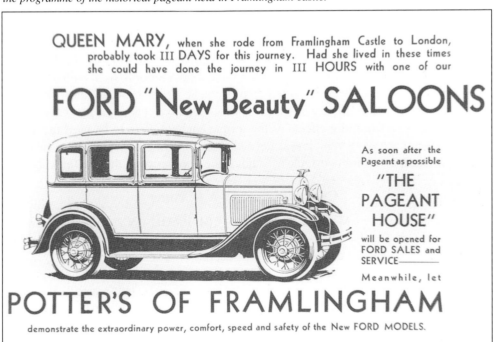

QUEEN MARY, when she rode from Framlingham Castle to London, probably took III DAYS for this journey. Had she lived in these times she could have done the journey in III HOURS with one of our

FORD "New Beauty" SALOONS

As soon after the Pageant as possible

"THE PAGEANT HOUSE"

will be opened for FORD SALES and SERVICE——

Meanwhile, let

POTTER'S OF FRAMLINGHAM

demonstrate the extraordinary power, comfort, speed and safety of the New FORD MODELS.

VISIT TO FORD WORKS
On MONDAY, June 18th, 1934
ARRANGED BY

A. H. POTTER, Woodbridge, and
A. G. POTTER (Framlingham) Ltd.

We have made arrangements for Saloon Coaches.

Leave Woodbridge 8. 5 a.m.
Leave Ipswich   ... 8.40 a.m.
Arrive Liverpool Street 10.24 a.m.

Proceed down Subway to Metropolitan Underground Railway.

Book single to **Westminster.**
Take any **Inner Circle** Train.

When we arrive at Westminster leave station and
cross road to **Westminster Bridge Pier.**

Board " New Dagenham" **before 11.30 a.m.**
at which time we leave for the Works. Lunch
has been arranged on board. When we get
to the Works guides will meet us, show us
round the Works and back to the boat. Tea
will be served on board on the return journey
and we arrive back at Westminster 5.30 p.m.

**We are due to leave Liverpool Street at
7.42 p.m.,** and that train on which the
saloon coaches will be reserved for us will
come right through to Woodbridge. There
is a later train leaving London at 10.25, but
it does not come back further than Ipswich,
arriving there at midnight. If you want
to stop till then please let Mr. H. Potter
know, as soon as possible, as we shall have
to arrange for a 'bus back to Woodbridge.

Travel arrangements for a day out to the Dagenham Works. With such detailed instructions there was little chance of getting lost en route.

Customers seeking a larger and more powerful car could still buy the Model B, introduced in 1932, and from 1935 the first of the 30hp V8 Fords were built at Dagenham, having previously been imported from Canada. From 1936, a 22hp V8 model was introduced, qualifying for a lower rate of taxation. These larger Fords were popular with A.G.'s farming clients as the torque enabled them to be used in various situations where a towing vehicle was needed. The following table, based on the company's purchasing requirements, clearly shows the popularity of the smaller cars.

Cars Purchased by A.G. Potter						
Year	Model Y	Model C	ABF	AB*	V8	V8
(Oct–Sept)	8hp	10hp	14.9hp	24hp	22hp	30hp
1932–33	10		5	2		3
1933–34	20		4			1
1935–36	32	15			10	4
1936–37	31	23			10	6

*AB was the official designation of the car commonly known as the Model B.

An interesting aside is how the motor car came to the assistance of the fire brigade, and this was well remembered by Morgan Watts. The hand-operated pump was originally drawn by horses lent by Mr Hatcher the coal merchant. Needless to say, certain delays occurred if a fire inconveniently happened at the same time as coal deliveries. The first advance came with the use of A.G.'s one-ton truck to haul the pump to the scene of the fire. But there was still the problem of getting the firemen there quickly, and the town council authorised A.G. to provide transport. Morgan performed this service with a Bean saloon, often arriving before the fire engine. In the mid-1930s A.G. bought a number of solid-tyred Dennis fire engines as a speculative venture. These were self-contained vehicles that could carry the fire crew, and had an engine-driven pump. The other fire engines were eventually sold to Debenham, Stradbroke, Aldeburgh, and Rochester in Kent.

Morgan set up his own cycle business in 1938, which was not a popular move as far as his former employer was concerned. Although he was able to obtain a joint agency with A.G. for BSA and Raleigh cycles, there was considerable competition between them. But as the cycle side of Potters business was by then declining, this presented a good opportunity for Morgan.

The outbreak of the Second World War saw many people being called up, and trade once again became very depressed. A.G. had the benefit of being involved with tractors and the essential production of food. Morgan Watts's cycle business was given a boost during the war years when the American 95th Bomb Group, shortly to be

The Ford 10 Model 7W, available between 1937 and 1939, was characterised by its bulging headlamps. This particular one, registration CRT62, has special significance as it was the author's place of birth, one winter's night in 1947, en route to hospital.

replaced by the 390th Bomb Group, arrived in 1943 at the newly constructed airbase at nearby Parham. With accommodation for some 3,000 people, the need for cheap personal transport was obvious, and many cycles were provided and repaired. They were an important currency, and on one occasion Morgan had to give evidence on valuations at a court martial, where military personnel were accused of stealing bicycles and selling them to new arrivals. During the war, he was on duty with the local ambulance corps, but reckoned any patient was more at risk from the exhaust fumes than the enemy, as the vehicles were in poor condition.

Potters were also dependent on work associated with the war effort, and serviced many of the lorries involved with the construction of the local air bases.

A.G. Potter died in 1942 at the age of 69. His son Jack took over the business, which has been an important employer in the town for many years. The firm celebrated its 80th year as a Ford dealer in 1993. The small road next to the original workshop was even called 'Potters Lane', unoficially, but, now all the buildings are gone, new generations will only know it as Brook Lane.

Morgan Watts died in 1986, aged 92. His early recollections were invaluable, and without them the author would never have been inspired to write this book.

CHAPTER SIX

SUFFOLK CAR MANUFACTURERS

Today the number of manufacturers in the country as a whole is very small, yet in the early years of this century over 220 firms are estimated to have entered the car production market. The majority of them had disappeared by around 1914. Suffolk had its fair share of enthusiasts who were set on building cars, but whether they can be considered as 'manufacturers' will, of course, depend on how you define the term, and the number of cars they produced in a year.

Most companies would have relied on bought-in engines and chassis, to which they added a body and all the ancillary systems. J.W. Brooke & Co Ltd were perhaps exceptional in that they also made their own engines and gearboxes. This company was without doubt the most important manufacturer and is covered here in some detail. Briefer descriptions of other Suffolk companies follow. Detailed research into all these firms is limited by a lack of company records. This chapter is mainly researched from period magazines, newspapers, show reports and catalogues, etc. As is to be expected, these tend to give a glowing description of the vehicles and there is little in the way of critical comment.

The following accounts are based on information discovered to date, and the author would be interested to hear of any further details or photographs.

J.W. Brooke & Co Ltd, Adrian Works, Alexandra Road, Lowestoft (1900–13)

John Walter Brooke moved to Lowestoft in 1874 at the age of 25, and took over a modest iron and brass foundry. The steady expansion of the business saw the construction of the Adrian Works, which eventually covered some 18,000 square feet.

Brooke became managing director when the firm was made a private limited company in 1897 and his son John Mawdsley, a prime influence in the move over to motoring, became works manager. Their first car was designed in 1900 with the co-operation of Ernest Estcourt, a leading motor engineer who became a director of the company and was to be heavily involved with the general development of Brooke cars. The introduction to their 1902 catalogue reads as follows:

> About a year ago it appeared to us that there was an opening for a good High-class Motor Carriage – a fast, good touring vehicle, but not a voiturette such as

(John) Mawdsley Brooke (1875–1957) was the main influence in leading the company into motor car production.

the market was being flooded with. With the object of designing such a carriage we set ourselves to work, examining cars of other manufacture, summarising their defects, and preparing drawings of what we anticipated would be an advance on the cars we had examined.

The Motor was the first detail to receive attention, with the result that we evolved one of three cyclinders, giving a constant 10-horsepower at 750 revolutions per minute with equal explosions over every two revolutions, the method of governing being by the throttling of the gases, the details of which were worked out in the year 1900, so that we feel that we may lay claim to being the pioneers in this system of governing in this Country.

During the process of completion of this Motor our attention was given to the Car itself, and more particularly to the system of transmission, our idea being to gain a greater efficiency in this gear than was obtainable by the usual method of high speed gear wheels, and more particularly 'Power Eating' bevel wheels.

The results we anticipated have been obtained, and we are now, in the beginning of 1902, in a position to offer a high-class, efficient, and quiet Motor-Carriage to the public.

Our works cover an area of 11,000 square feet, employ on an average 100 men, and consist of Pattern-making Shops, Iron, Brass and Aluminium Foundries, Smithy, Machine Shops, and a large Assembling Floor, the whole being, together with the General and Drawing Offices, on the Ground Floor, with the exception of Galleries in the main Machine Shop, for light work. The different departments are arranged for the production of work on the interchangeable principle and in quantities. The Machine Shops are replete with modern and up-to-date Tools suitable for dealing with this special class of work; the Foundries, Smithy and Pattern Shop being equipped in a similar manner.

The prototype of their first car had no doors, and the rear passengers had to climb over the front seats, all of which were fully exposed to the elements. When it went into production, in 1902, a three-cylinder transversely-mounted water-cooled engine propelled the car at 25–30mph. The steering wheel was of novel design – with a steel dish instead of spokes – and could accommodate maps and gloves etc, and had an oilskin cover. In chassis form the car cost £305, rising to £420 for a double phaeton with removable back seat. The War Office was among their first customers.

Mr Albert Murton, editor of the *Lowestoft Journal*, was taken for a run in the car by Mawdsley Brooke and Estcourt, and gave the following account of it.

> It is now generally recognised, except by the fossilised, that motor cars have come to stay. The raising of the speed limit to 12mph is one step in the right direction, although an inadequate one. The absurd prejudice against them is breaking down; it is now proposed to raise the limit to 20mph.
>
> Mr Mawdsley Brooke, who is well known as an enthusiastic motorist has made a deep study of the subject and, as a result, a motor car has been evolved which, in the opinion of the experts who are qualified to judge, is far advanced both in construction and speed of anything of its size. The car was timed at 25mph despite the conditions of the roads. Coachwork was well executed by P. Watson & Sons, St Peter's Street. There is thus every possibility of a new and lucrative industry for Lowestoft. Brooke & Co have carried out big contracts for the Admiralty, War and India Offices, the London Schools and Metropolitan Asylum Boards. It is confidently expected that, great as has been the progress of Adrian Works in the past, they will be even more so in the future with the development of the motor car business.

As the Brooke company was already well established, with extensive engineering works, they were in a good position to manufacture the many parts necessary for their

Mawdsley Brooke with the first three-cylinder car in 1902. Note the dished steering wheel which doubled up as a glove/map compartment.

own car. They were the only Suffolk motor firm to produce engines, with castings from their own foundry. The Zephyr of later years, also from Lowestoft, can be discounted as it never went into production.

The three-cylinder engines were transversely mounted and fitted with Estcourt's patent automatic intake valve. The company admitted that the dashboard was of unusual construction in order to accommodate the engine cooler, yet another Estcourt patent, which did not rely on the use of a water pump. The transmission was via chain to the gearbox, and finally by chain to the rear wheel. The gearbox itself was unusual in that it had internal chain drive.

The 1903 Crystal Palace Exhibition in January saw two 12hp models exhibited: a tonneau at £445 and a limousine at £600, both powered by a three-cylinder engine. They were claimed to be 'perfectly silent, vibrationless and noted for their hill climbing powers'. The latter was tested in Automobile Club Reliability Trials where they were able to climb hills 'without shedding passengers'. One month later, a new longitudinal 14hp three-cylinder car, with three forward speeds and a reverse, was announced. Initially, the price was £445, but this soon increased to £500.

The relative cost of most cars was high, and facilities for spreading the payments were necessary to increase the number of sales. The Brooke cars were sold through several companies, one of them being Rolls & Co of West Brompton. The Brooke car was one of thirty-six different makes offered on an instalment plan, with 5 per cent being added to the list prices.

A new development occurred when Brooke experimented with two 15hp engines doubled up to form their first six-cylinder engine, which was tested in a motor launch in 1903. This was some time before S.F. Edge's Napier company put Britain's first six-cylinder-engined car on the road.

By 1904 the firm had produced a more conventional 15–20hp four-cylinder in-line engine, fitted with governors operated by the carburettor suction. Ignition was by high- and low-tension magneto, and final drive from the gearbox by chain. This model appears to have been popular, as one advertisement made reference to it having been out of stock owing to excessive demand. Approximately 75 per cent of the company's business was related to motor car production in this period.

The next year saw the introduction of a 35hp four-cylinder car. Various reports on the car in the motoring press gave the bore and stroke as 5.5 inches (140mm) and 6 inches (152mm) respectively, giving a capacity of 9,344cc. The Brooke catalogue however, quotes 6.5 inches (165mm) and 7 inches (178mm), which would provide a massive capacity of 15,225cc. These figures appear to relate to a period before the car was actually available and the lower capacity is more likely to have been correct. There was much discussion in the motoring press of the time concerning the merits of four- and six-cylinder engines. In January 1906, Mawdsley Brooke wrote to *The Autocar* saying that although he could cater for four or six cylinders, he had a notion that only the latter would be available in a year's time. His new 25hp six-cylinder car was ready for delivery in April of that year, and was the first Brooke with live axle.

S.F. Edge was one of the most prominent motoring pioneers and a very accom-

The four-cylinder Brooke, introduced in 1904, had a more conventional in-line engine. This landaulette version would have cost around £650.

plished salesman too. His own company S.F. Edge Ltd was already selling the six-cylinder Napier when the new Brooke car was launched. He presumably saw an opportunity to corner the market as he bought up all the first year's production. *The Autocar* in January 1907 made the following comments on the Brooke:

> The chosen of S. F. Edge Ltd as a six-cylinder second string would be expected to be found as good as could be, and in partly riding and partly driving this car from London to Guildford and back over the far famed Portsmouth Road, we were emphatically of the opinion that, so far as this car went, the expert had not been guilty of any error of judgement.

The 1907 Brooke catalogue gives the standard finish as 'Napier green, with nickel plated fittings and green leather upholstery'. The new model was captioned 'The Car of Silent Speed' and described by the company as follows:

> Do you know the 'Brooke' Car? If you do not, and are not aware of its many good points, may we try and interest you in the following description of what we believe to be one of the most perfect cars on the market?
>
> It is fitted with a six-cylinder engine developing 30hp, embracing many special features fully bearing out the reputation of the 'Brooke' Cars as regards absolute reliability, simplicity in design and construction, ease of control and low price, and this for what is undoubtedly a triumph of English workmanship, excelling in many ways anything hitherto produced.

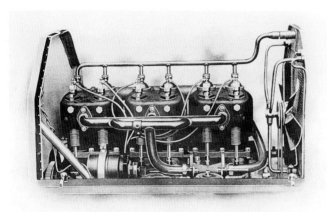

Brooke were developing a six-cylinder engine in 1903, but it was to be another three years before the car was launched into a competitive marketplace.

The engine has six cylinders, cast in pairs, and develops 30hp at 1,000rpm. It is newly and carefully designed, runs with absolute smoothness, and vibration is conspicuous by its absence. This we venture to point out must commend itself to up-to-date Motorists. Another and most important point is that it picks up the load immediately and without hesitation, and the flexibility of the Engine gives a wide range of speeds without changing the gears.

The 'Brooke' Cars have always held a reputation for quietness in running and in this new Car the reputation has been maintained.

The gearbox is a very simple piece of mechanism. Here, as everywhere else in this Car, we have avoided all complications, thus securing a durability and certainty of action rarely seen in the usual gearbox. Four speeds and reverse are provided instead of the usual three speeds forward and reverse, but you should note that the direct drive is on the third, not on the top speed. It is the third speed that you will use most of the time, the fourth being required occasionally when great speed is essential, or when everything is in your favour for a good run.

On the third speed you can climb most hills quite easily, and yet do over 40 miles an hour on the level, so that it is a distinct advantage to have the through drive on this speed, and so avoid unnecessary friction. It may be mentioned here that the change speed gear is actuated through a gate, and has a spring engagement which ensures absolute silence when changing speeds.

The next consideration is that of the Brakes, one of the most vital parts of the Car. They are exceptionally powerful and *can be relied upon* to hold the Car on any hill. It is needless to dilate on this most important point. Briefly, they are all metal to metal, the foot brake operating on a drum at the back of the gearbox. The hand brakes expand internally in drums carried on the back wheel axle boxes, and actuated through the side and levers.

The wheels on the 'Brooke' Car are all 34-inch diameter, the front wheels being shod with 870 x 90mm tyres, and the back wheels with 880 x 120mm tyres. This is a fact worth remembering when you are buying a Car.

The body is most luxurious and comfortable, constructed with wood frames and aluminium panels, side entrance, five-seated and spacious; the leather upholstery is of the highest class, making altogether a most elegant, comfortable and one of the smoothest running British Cars on the market.

An extract from the *Motor Car Journal* of June 23rd, 1906 would here not be out of place. 'Reclining in the six-cylinder "Brooke" Car, with its easy armchair tonneau was a real delight; no vibration, nor jarring notes, no cramped limbs, just such a Car as one can spend a day in without discomfort.'

The fact should not be lost sight of that the price for this six-cylinder Car is extremely low, viz., for the side entrance complete Car to standard specification, £650, painted and upholstered to client's own wishes. This price includes complete outfit of tools, spare parts, double twist horn, two side lamps and regulation tail lamp, repair outfit, pump and rubber mats.

Although we claim that everything that is possible to make a breakdown unknown has been done, still in cases of accident or wear from long use, it is useful to know that every part of the 'Brooke' Car has been standardised, and that renewals can be obtained immediately from the makers' stores at Lowestoft.

If you will allow us the opportunity of giving you a trial run we are sure you will be charmed, and we should be at any time most willing to show you over the Works at Lowestoft, where you can see for yourself the 'Brooke Car of Silent Speed', under construction by the newest and most perfect machines, and under ideal conditions.

A 40hp six-cylinder chassis was introduced in 1907, with a rudimentary body consisting of side doors to two seats in the front and three in the back, with individual hoods for inclement weather. Mawdsley Brooke's notion about his six-cylinder cars was correct, as all four-cylinder-engine production was then discontinued.

In 1908 the company took stock of the situation with regard to the production of motor cars, and decided that it was not possible to keep up the high development costs that were needed to produce new models for an ever demanding market. The 25 and 40hp models were last exhibited at the Olympia show in November 1908.

BJ504 was a 40hp model, reviewed by the motoring press in 1908. Various members of the Brooke family pose with the new car while out for a drive in the country.

Mawdsley Brooke in a later 40hp car outside the Wherry Hotel, Oulton Broad, c. 1910.

Meanwhile, the marine side of the business was rapidly developing, and in 1911 four acres of land with river frontage were purchased. Two years later the company employed over 300 men. Mawdsley, in a speech that year, referred to orders for ten motor boats for the Admiralty, a launch for the King of Greece, a motor tug for the Sudan Government, launches for a Russian and an Austrian Count, and several motors. They were clearly concentrating on the marine market and this was probably the last year in which any cars were produced. However, in their relatively short period of production, the company had become well established and managed to secure several notable customers.

There was considerable variation between the types and makes of car available to the public, and the only way to be sure of what you were buying was to road test an example. The author Max Pemberton was keen to try one of the Brooke cars, but only a bare chassis model was available. A temporary cover was placed over the engine and an open seat fitted to the chassis. The test run to Cambridge and back was successfully completed, with the return journey being on the following day. The car must have been to Mr Pemberton's satisfaction as he promptly placed an order for it, to be completed by the coach-builders with a folding hood – though this would still have left the driver and front passenger unprotected.

The strangest vehicle produced by this company must have been the Swan car. Mr Robert Nicoll 'Scotty' Matthewson, a wealthy Scottish engineer of Swan Park, Alipore, Calcutta, took three years to design and build the body, which was magnificently carved with the head, tail and feathers of a swan. This was then shipped to Lowestoft to be fitted onto a Brooke chassis with six-cylinder engine. A photograph of the completed car appeared in the 2 March 1910 edition of *The Car*.

Monty Blake, a fitter for Brooke's, was 'lent' to Mr Matthewson for six months while the car was being completed, and found him a trifle eccentric.

> We had to fit all sorts of gadgets to the car. There was a Gabriel horn with eight organ pipes, and a keyboard with a two-way valve system operated by the exhaust when the old gentleman decided to have a tune. You passed the exhaust

pressure through the Gabriel horn and you could play anything within the range of its eight notes. The swan's head had red and amber prisms for eyes which lit up at night.

There was also a lever that opened the swan's beak and another lever sent half a pint of water from the radiator pipes into the swan's nostrils. A compressed air cylinder then forced the water out of the nostrils with a hissing sound. One day, before we had the electric starter, the chaps at the Works pushed us off and we drove to St Olaves where we stopped for lunch at the Bell. Mr Matthewson was so pleased that we cracked a bottle of champagne. Another day, we drove to Norwich and pulled up in The Walk. We played a tune on the horn and I operated the lever forcing water out of the swan's nostrils. While the crowd were looking at us open-mouthed and somewhat damp I was ordered to drive off.

After successful trials around Lowestoft, the Swan was shipped out to India, where it was an even greater sensation. The car caused such a stir on the streets of Calcutta that it was eventually banned by the police, and disappeared from public view, seemingly forever. It therefore came as a great surprise when rumours circulated in 1991 that the Swan was back in this country. These rumours were proved correct when the car was put up for auction and realised the sum of £170,000. It was most rewarding to see this unique vehicle, with its Suffolk-built chassis and engine, after reading so many stories about it. The name Brooke is clearly cast on the exhaust manifold, float chamber and foot pedals, while the year 1910 is stamped on the cylinder head. A Cygnet car was also offered for auction at the same time, and sold for £9,000. Constructed as a miniature of the Swan, it was powered by a now-missing electric motor. The Swan has since been restored in Britain by Jerry Brett of Prowess Racing (Restoration) Ltd.

Scotty Matthewson with his recently completed Swan car, at the Brooke factory, 1910. This car still exists and has recently been the subject of a major restoration (see also back cover).

Another Brooke curiosity was a four-cylinder model owned by Sydney Walton, a Lowestoft brewer. When extra power was required he would operate a lever to open a port in the exhaust leading to the silencer. At night, this made an impressive sight with flames shooting out, while the crack of the exhaust gave it a sense of great power.

On one occasion, however, Mr Walton somehow managed to drive his car from Lowestoft to Malvern, Worcestershire, with no oil in the sump. Although all the bearings were worn out, the engine survived, and after reconditioning it went back into service again. This car, registration AH 88, was loaned to the Post Office in 1905 to help with the Christmas mail, and in 1911 took Boy Scouts to their annual camp at Long Stratton. It was in use throughout the First World War and not scrapped until the 1920s. Even after that, the engine continued to power a chaff cutter for many years.

The Brooke cars were undoubtedly well made and built to last. After several years of service, one of their six-cylinder 40hp models was converted into a motor hearse – with dark-coloured waterproof curtains instead of glass panels. At the end of its useful life as a hearse it was used by the local fish merchant for delivering his wares to surrounding areas.

St John Nixon, in *The Antique Automobile*, makes reference to the Brooke cars.

> Several different models were made, but the Brooke car was one of those that failed to survive. It performed well in most of the trials in which it competed, but at that time it was a very uphill task to popularise a British-made car. Much money was expended in experimental work for the purpose of improving the breed; it was also advertised very widely, but it never caught the public imagination.

The following list was compiled from various sources, which do not always agree with each other. However, it does provide a fair representation of the models available and their typical costs. Unfortunately no record remains of the number of vehicles produced. In 1904 the company auctioned ten new three-cylinder models, with stated chassis numbers up to 040. As they continued to produce cars for several more years, J.W. Brooke & Co Ltd can be clearly identified as the most important manufacturer in Suffolk.

Brooke Cars 1902–1913

1902	10hp	*Three-cylinder*	
		Chassis	£305
		Tonneau or Single Phaeton	£395
		Double Phaeton	£420
1903–5	12hp	*Three-cylinder*	
		Capacity 2,398cc	
		Chassis	£335
		Tonneau	£400–450
		Light Car	£450
		Limousine	£540–600

1903–4	14hp	*Three-cylinder*	
		Capacity 2,875cc	
		Tonneau	£445–500
		Limousine	£600
1903	15hp	*Three-cylinder*	
		Capacity 3,213cc	
1904–7	15–20hp	*Four-cylinder*	
		Capacity 3,213cc	
		Short Chassis	£490
		Long Chassis	£510
		Tonneau	£550
		Landaulette	£650
1905–7	35hp	*Four-cylinder*	
		Capacity 9,344cc	
		Side Entrance	£750
1906–13	25–30hp	*Six-cylinder*	
		Capacity 4,788cc	
1907		Chassis	£685
		Landaulette	£820
		Limousine	£850
1911–13	38hp	*Six-cylinder*	
		Capacity 6,000cc	
1907–13	40hp	*Six-cylinder*	
		Capacity 6,516cc	

Other Suffolk companies are now covered in alphabetical order. Where only a basic listing is given, this is from *Kelly's Directory*, and should not be taken as proof that any cars were actually made. It is possible that some of these firms produced coachwork for other manufacturers' chassis, or assembled cars from imported engines and local parts. If they had been involved in any significant manufacture, no doubt a better record of their existence would have survived.

Anglian Cycle & Engineering Co Ltd, Anglian Works, Stowmarket

The firm of Stannard & Alger was in business in 1896 as mechanical engineers and cycle makers. By around 1900 Richard Stannard was proprietor of the Anglian Cycle & Engineering Co, electroplaters and enamellers, manufacturers of dynamos, motors and cycles. This trading name was dropped by 1904, and the company continued thereafter as Stannard & Co, claiming to be sole makers of 'Anglian' cycles and motors. The firm produced a quadricycle, advertised as the ideal doctors' vehicle, which could be converted to a tricycle in fifteen minutes. No other details have been

The Anglian Motor Co Ltd of Beccles sold a wide range of cars, but only the smaller De Dion-powered cars were of their own manufacture. Superintendent John Newson of Beccles received an annual allowance in 1909 for using this 8hp Anglian on official business, with his driver PC Eade.

found in relation to car production, and two-wheeled vehicles appear to have been their mainstay. There is no apparent connection between this company and the following one of similar name. The reference to 'sole' makers of Anglian cycles and motors hints at resentment of a similarly-named product.

Anglian Motor Co Ltd, Station Road and Newgate Street, Beccles

William Robinson started his own general engineering and cycle manufacturing business in the 1890s. He was the first person to own a motor car in Beccles, and clearly saw the potential of the new form of transport. In August 1903 major developments took place when he formed a limited company, with the new directors providing capital to expand into motorcar sales and, hopefully, to produce a car of their own manufacture.

The Anglian Motor Co Ltd had the following directors:

> Honourable A.J. Mulholland of Worlingham Hall, Chairman
> Charles Wilson, MP for Hull
> Captain S. Saunderson, Managing Director
> A. Saunderson, Agent to Worlingham Hall Estate
> W. Robinson, General Director and Works Manager

At this time there was a staff of twenty, which continued to produce their own 'Clifton' motor cycles with De Dion engines. The firm also obtained various car agencies. By the end of 1903, they had secured the UK agency for the French Aries car, and were exhibiting at the Crystal Palace Show.

William Robinson was a keen promoter of motorised transport, and in the following year held the 8th annual show of his various products. Crowded into the Public Hall at Beccles were a great number of bicycles, eight No 1 Anglian motorcycles, two of the latest No 2 models, two Trimo's and various types of trailer. They had to remove the Hall doors to allow the 10hp Aries in, but the rest of the cars had to stay outside. The car of their own manufacture – a two-seater with a 6hp De Dion single-cylinder engine – also made an appearance. A novel feature was the fold-out rear passenger seat compartment that could alternatively be used to store luggage. This was a forerunner of the dickey seat that was to be popular in later years. The cost of the Anglian was £150, compared with £400 for the Aries, and several orders were taken for it. The company claimed to be the only one in England to hold a stock of the De Dion engines as used in the Anglian. How much of the car was of their manufacture is unknown as it was common for companies to buy in components such as bonnets, radiators, etc, in order to make their own car.

For 1905 there was a London showroom in Basil Street, and cars were exhibited at Olympia. These had Aster engines fitted, the largest being a 15hp model with four cylinders and chain drive to the wheels. (Aster engines were manufactured near the Aries factory in France.) Later in the year, the Duke of Newcastle purchased an Anglian with a 20hp Aster engine and an extra long chassis. The side-entrance double phaeton body was built by Norwich coachbuilders W. & F. Thorn, and was finished off with silver-plated fittings.

Anglian Cars 1905		
6hp	One-cylinder	£185
9hp	One-cylinder	£200
8–10hp	Two-cylinder	£235–280 (four models)
10–12hp	Two-cylinder	£300–320 (two models)
12hp	Two-cylinder	£400
15hp	Four-cylinder	£550–650 (three models)
20hp	Four-cylinder	£600
28hp	Four-cylinder	£750

Although they were all referred to as Anglians, the larger models were of Aries origin. A reduced range was available in early 1906, but after then the Anglian name is no longer seen in manufacturers' listings. It is therefore unlikely that there was further production, and the company appeared to rely on agencies such as Hallamshire and Daimler.

By around 1912, the company reverted to the name of William Robinson of the Anglian Motor Works, and continued to trade as motor engineers for many years.

Durrants Motors Ltd, Horn Hill, Mill Road, Lowestoft
Listed as a manufacturer in 1904.

James, Talbot & Davison (1916) Ltd, Freemantle Road, Lowestoft
This Lowestoft company, like Brooke, intended to manufacture their own engines, but serious production never started. Their prototype car was called the Zephyr, and was reviewed in several publications after the war. The following account, from *The Motor* in April 1920, well describes this interesting car.

The 1920 Zephyr Car

It is not unusual to find that manufacturers of some component part of a chassis make at some time or other in their own works a complete car for the purpose of thoroughly testing their own particular component. This is the case with the Zephyr car. Originally designed and built in 1913 for the purpose of testing the Zephyr patent pistons, prior to the war the car was undergoing strenuous tests, the results of which were markedly successful; so successful, in fact, that plant was put down and provisions made for production on a large scale in 1915.

As was the case with so many best-laid plans, the war intervened and the whole of the works of James Talbot and Davison Ltd, of Lowestoft, were placed at the disposal of the Government, a very large number of aero engines and other munitions being manufactured. During this period, however, the experimental car was running practically continuously under war service conditions, and, although all energies were concentrated on output of other machines, the time spent proved that the car was a reliable and satisfactory proposition.

Government contracts being now completed, the plant and organisation of the works at Lowestoft have been turned over altogether to the production of the complete car. The policy of the concern is to provide owner-drivers with a car which is complete in itself and which incorporates the capabilities for hard work with long life and ease of upkeep.

With a bore and stroke of 69 mm x 130 mm the four cylinders of the engine are cast en bloc and are provided with a detachable head. With the object of obtaining a flexible unit the cylinder block is set desaxé over the crankshaft, reducing side thrust on the cylinder walls and thereby conserving power and minimizing wear. Overhead valves enclosed by an easily detachable dust-proof cover are fitted. All the tappets are adjustable, and accessibility has been specially studied. Internally the same high-class specification continues; the crankshaft is forged from heat- treated steel, each rotating part being balanced in its own plane, thus eliminating any possibility of periodic vibration and undue wear on bearings. Naturally, Zephyr patent pistons are fitted. These pistons have been used with great success in aero engines, and were fitted to the Vickers-Vimy which the late Capt Sir John Alcock flew across the Atlantic, as well as to the machine which Sir Ross Smith flew from London to Australia. Little else need be said as proof of their efficiency. Unit construction of the gearbox is adopted, the drive being taken from the engine through a cone-type Ferodo-lined clutch, while four speeds are provided, operating by a central control lever working in a gate. As to the rest of the engine, it will be sufficient to say that the high tension magneto is placed where it can be easily cleaned and adjusted; a

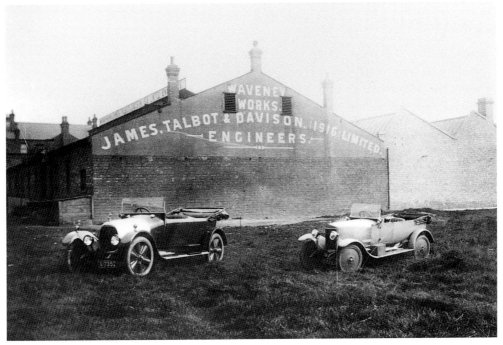

James Talbot & Davison Ltd of Lowestoft developed the Zephyr car. It was extensively reviewed by several motoring journals in 1920 but failed to reach quantity production. The car on the right is a Zenith, the other an Angus Sanderson.

Zenith carburettor is fitted; cooling is by thermo-syphonic circulation; and lubrication is by combined forced feed and splash.

On a high-class car such as the Zephyr one would naturally expect to find cantilever rear springs, and this is the case.

Following modern practice, the radiator is pointed, and only one door is fitted to the body, the two front seats being separate to provide a passage-way to the rear seats. The provisional chassis price is £400 complete.

A subsequent report stated: 'The production programme for the Zephyr car has been somewhat upset by difficulties in obtaining material supplies, particularly cylinder castings. Production should go ahead as soon as all the necessary material is available. This is certainly one of the most promising of the after-war productions.'

Four or five of these cars were apparently built but full-scale production was never reached, due to difficulties in obtaining the cylinder blocks in this country. A Belgian firm did start to produce them, but they suffered from porosity problems and this was presumably a major reason why the car did not go into production.

Fortunately, though, the engineering side of the business continued, and the firm of Zephyr Cams descended from the original company.

S.J. Jenkins Ltd, Risbygate Garage, Bury St Edmunds

Listed as a manufacturer from 1912.

The 6hp Lindsay voiturette of 1905 had a JAP engine which powered the car through a variable-drive mechanism. It cost £140 and had brakes on all four wheels, an unusual feature for this period.

Lindsay Motor Manufacturing Company Ltd, Ipswich Road, Woodbridge (1905–8)

Mr John Lindsay Scott originally produced tricars in London. These machines had an interesting drive mechanism called the Low's variable gear, consisting of two fixed flanges on a drum, and a third movable flange between them. A hand-operated lever enabled the diameter of the pulleys to be infinitely varied, and at the same time maintained the belt tension. The car was powered by a 4hp engine and had a wickerwork carriage in front.

By 1905 the company had moved on to car production in Woodbridge with the manufacture of a 6hp voiturette with JAP engine in a tubular-steel frame. A cone clutch was again used to transmit power to the Low's variable drive, with chains to the rear wheel. An unusual feature for a car of this period was the use of brakes on all four wheels. It claimed to cover 40 miles on one gallon of petrol. A year later, a 12hp car with a four-cylinder Fafnir engine was introduced. Significant changes had occurred in the transmission department as a three-speed gearbox was used, along with shaft drive to the rear axle. Perhaps the variable gearing had not been able to take the increased power of the larger engine. A 28–35hp car with an Antoine engine, selling at £470, was also introduced. The final model, in 1908, had a 1.8-litre short-stroke four-cylinder engine rated at 15.9hp.

The company went into liquidation later that same year, with Mr Parkes and Mr Pullen, the foreman and works manager, joining forces to start their own general engineering company.

The Lindsay premises were purpose-built at Barrack Corner, and are still in use for the sale of motor cars. The roof outline of the original building can still be seen.

Lindsay Cars 1904–1908

1904	4hp	Two-cylinder	Tricar	
1905	6hp	Two-cylinder JAP	Voiturette	£140
1906	12hp	Four-cylinder Fafnir	Phaeton de Luxe	£252
	20hp	Four-cylinder	Belgian built	£470
	28–30hp	Four-cylinder Antoine		£530
1907	15hp	Four-cylinder		£270
	20hp	Four-cylinder		£470
	30hp	Four-cylinder		£530
1908	16hp	Four-cylinder	Side entrance	£350
		Brougham		£395
		Landaulette		£405

In addition to the above models, other types have been noted, such as the 10hp model driven by Mrs Lindsay Scott in tests at Sudbourne Park and Lawford Hill in 1907; also, BJ436 and BJ755, which were registered as 7–9hp cars.

There is inevitably some uncertainty over the exact models and the periods when they were produced.

Parr & Bryant, Ingate, Beccles
Listed as a manufacturer in 1916.

1908 was the final year of production for Lindsay, when the range was rationalised to the 16hp model only.

115

The Lindsay Motor Manufacturing Co Ltd produced cars at these premises in Woodbridge between 1905 and 1908.

Smith & Co, East Suffolk Carriage Works, Halesworth

A note in Lambert's Almanac for 1909 says: 'The East Suffolk Carriage Works, noted in recent years for the excellence of its carriages, has kept itself abreast of the times by turning its attention to the building of motor cars.' From then until 1914 the business flourished, with much overtime, but was then badly affected by the outbreak of war.

Thoroughfare Motors Ltd, Woodbridge

This firm started business in the Thoroughfare in 1912 as agents for R.C.H cars. The following year they reopened the old Lindsay works at Barrack Corner, renaming it 'The Ridley Motor Works'. From these premises they manufactured the Ridley Carette, which was described in the *Light Car and Cyclecar* of 1914 as follows:

> **Thoro'fare Motors, Ltd.**
> **RIDLEY WORKS,** Ipswich Road,
> **SHOWROOMS,** The Thoro'fare,
> WOODBRIDGE.
>
> R.C.H., Overland, Hurtu, Ford,
> And any make of car supplied promptly.
>
> MANUFACTURERS OF THE
> **RIDLEY CARETTE**

The Ridley was advertised locally by Thoroughfare Motors Ltd in 1914.

The Ridley Carette was manufactured in the old Lindsay Works in 1914 and sold for £135. Its twin-cylinder engine operated through a friction transmission via a belt-drive to the rear wheels.

The first impression of the Ridley Carette is that it is a car in miniature. The domed wings, with metal extensions, the coach-built body, and the rubber-covered running boards would seem to imply an expensive car. But the Ridley is constructed on the simplest lines, every endeavour being made to combine reliable construction and simplicity of design with a low first cost. The frame is of pressed steel, carried at the front on half-elliptic springs, and at the rear on three-quarter elliptics. This combination should produce very easy riding and great comfort.

The engine, a twin-cylinder Blumfield cyclecar engine, as is well known, is provided with mechanical lubrication. An automatic carburettor, with both foot and hand control, is fitted, while the firing point of the high-tension magneto is variable.

Incorporated with the flywheel is a sliding joint, to allow for the dis-engagement of the discs. A short length of propeller shaft carries the driving disc at the rear, while the driven disc is faced with compressed paper, and can be moved along the counter-shaft to allow of changes of gear. The final drive is by rubber belts running over large solid pulleys on the countershaft. No trouble whatever should be anticipated in this direction, as the belts are running under practically ideal conditions.

On the countershaft is mounted a band brake, operated by pedal, while the side lever operates shoe brakes inside the rear belt rims. Steering is on large car lines, a neat worm and sector gear being fitted. Mounted on the steering column are two levers, one for spark and the other for throttle.

The body is very solidly constructed and ample room is provided for two persons. The standard equipment includes a hood, a screen, two acetylene headlights and generator, paraffin side and tail lamps, tools, jacks, etc. The price is £135 and the makers are Messrs Thoroughfare Motors Ltd, Ridley Works, Woodbridge, Suffolk.

By 1914, the company advertised that they had a London showroom, at Messrs Pellants Ltd, 74 Shaftesbury Avenue. It is not clear what happened to the business, but it probably ceased to trade effectively due to lack of orders and the fact that many employees had gone off to the war. The Ridley Works were, in fact, later used as a prisoner of war camp.

The Woodbridge Engineering Co Ltd

Following the Armistice and the slow demob of the soldiers, many businesses were reactivated and new ones started. One estimate put the figure for new companies proposing to produce cars in 1919 at forty. Full details of the Woodbridge Engineering Co Ltd, manufacturer of the Suffolk Royal, are unknown. The following account is based on newspaper details and discussions with Jimmy Postans, who worked for Thoroughfare Motors before the war, when it was run by a Mr Wrentmore.

In April 1919, this full-page advertisement appeared in the *Woodbridge Reporter*.

The Woodbridge Engineering Co Ltd
Directors John Williams MP, Lt Col Collen,
Wm Wrentmore, Managing Director,
beg to announce the reopening of the Ridley Works,
lately occupied by the military authorities, and known as
the 'Prisoners of War Camp'.
These works will be utilised entirely for motor car manufacture
and motor repairs. The Woodbridge Motor Works in the
Thoroughfare will remain open for the sale of
accessories supplies and repairs.

In the following weeks their promotions were mainly related to agricultural engineering matters as they were selling Beeman tractors. By October 1919, the company was also trading from the St Johns Works, which had previously been occupied by Alfred Adams for his motor and cycle business.

The first mention of the Suffolk Royal occurs in the advertisements of January 1920, when they were also trying to impress potential purchasers: 'Our consulting engineer holds the highest possible qualifications, BSc, MIME, etc.'

This must have been a period of great excitement for the company, with the prospect of a high quality car being produced shortly. The make-up of the board of directors does not seem typical of a small-town motor works, and this was further extended in April when a Major Richardson DSO of Pitfour Castle joined the board. The *Woodbridge Reporter* recorded these general notes and quoted: 'Mr John Williams MP has consented to act as Chairman of the above Public Company, now in course of flotation.'

The last advertisement appeared only two months later, on 3 June 1920. In just over a year, this high-profile company seems to have risen and sunk without trace, except for the advertising literature for the Suffolk Royal. It is understood that two of the directors resigned from the company, which must have precipitated its demise. Potter & Bensley (see Chapter 5) started trading from the St Johns Motor Works in 1921, and the Fawn Motor Syndicate Ltd of Stratford St Mary were to carry on motor car and van manufacture at the Ridley Works.

Jimmy Postans's recollections would suggest that the Woodbridge Engineering Co Ltd was a post-war revival of Thoroughfare Motors, with Mr Wrentmore being a common element. The Royal had a six-cylinder overhead camshaft engine, produced by the Sage Company, who started engine manufacture after the Armistice.

The main question is whether any Royals were actually manufactured. Jimmy Postans saw one in chassis form at the Barrack Corner Works, with enough parts around to complete another one or two. They went away to have bodies fitted, but he did not see them again. Were it not for the survival of the Royal advertising material, the name would not be known at all today. However, from the lack of recorded information, and the short existence of the company, it is reasonable to assume they were not made in any significant numbers. The claims for the car were as follows:

THE 'SUFFOLK ROYAL'

This Car has been designed in collaboration with some of the foremost Engine and Chassis designers of modern times as a perfect machine in every detail. It embraces the latest and best of modern automobile practice.

The Engine, rated at 15.64hp by the Royal Automobile Club Formula, has a reserve of power unsurpassed by any other Motor Car Engine of similar rating. It is quite the best and most efficient power unit that it is possible to produce.

The whole Car has been designed, built, and standardised since the Armistice. It is not a cheap mass-production proposition. Although it has been designed in every line with 'Production' in view, nothing has been scamped so as to reduce cost of production. In result, we offer a Car of superfine quality, capable of doing any amount of the hardest work.

Service in France proved the value in time saving by the use of the Warland Rims. A Lady, unassisted, can change a tyre with ease.

The 'Suffolk Royal' Car is known as the 'Forsyth' Model, or 'Model F'. Our guarantee to Owners of the Suffolk Royal Cars, who insure under our special assurance arrangements, is really worthy of your consideration.

After the First World War, the Woodbridge Engineering Co Ltd proposed to manufacture the Suffolk Royal in the old Lindsay Works. It was advertised in 1920, but the company failed soon after and few are likely to have been produced.

Two well-known Ipswich companies also became involved with the motor car, albeit in a very small way. **E.R. & F. Turner Ltd,** who manufactured milling equipment, were requested to produce a car for one of their clients in 1908. That model was a 35hp six-cylinder 'Orleans'. There was an Orleans Motor Co Ltd in Twickenham between 1905 and 1910, whose products were based on a Belgian Car. A 35hp six-cylinder model was available from 1907, and contemporary photographs show it to be virtually identical to the Turner car. It is thought that they manufactured about six cars under licence around this period, although none was registered in Ipswich.

Ransomes Sims & Jefferies Ltd manufactured a number of electric trucks after the First World War, and in 1920 they registered a Milburn electric car, DX2274. From the photographs, this appears to be a standard Milburn electric car from America. As no company details exist regarding this particular vehicle, it is unclear whether they were evaluating it, or whether it was fitted with one of their own motors. An electric motor cycle was also produced in 1919. This was an experimental model as the motor was fitted in a Rudge-Whitworth frame.

There is an interesting connection between Suffolk and one of America's most prestigious car manufacturers. In 1638 Samuel and Elizabeth **Packard** left Whitsun Green, Stonham Aspal, and sailed for America in the SS Diligent from Ipswich. James Ward Packard and his brother William, descendants of these early emigrants, bought their first car in 1898. They were not happy with this vehicle and decided they could do better. In 1900 they produced the first Packard, in Warren, Ohio. The firm was noted for its quality cars, the last one leaving the production line in 1958.

Between 1908 and 1910, some Orleans cars appear to have been made under licence by E.R. & F. Turner Ltd of Ipswich. This 1908 model was a considerable departure from the manufacture of milling equipment, which was their main line of business.

CHAPTER SEVEN

MOTOR HIRE

The public's first real contact with the motor car often came through hiring, and most motor businesses had vehicles available for this purpose, with or without driver. For example, by 1912, there were at least three firms in Framlingham able to offer such services, and the competition was keen. Charles Garrard's hire book provides several interesting entries.

1908

3 June	Her Grace The Duchess of Hamilton.		
	To Felixstowe Show for one day.	£2 2s 0d	(£2.10)
11 July	The Marquis of Graham.		
	To Ipswich cricket match and Saxmundham station.	£2 10s 0d	(£2.50)

1909

12 Nov	E. Suffolk Education Committee (Elementary). Hire of Argyll car and driver to Monk Soham, Worlingworth, Bedfield, Saxtead and Wickham Market station.	£1 2s 6d	(£1.125)
14 Nov	Conservative Association. Hire of Argyll car and driver from 2.30–11.30pm.	£2 2s 0d	(£2.10)

1910

19 Aug	E. Cocks. Hire of Argyll and driver for tour, 5–19 August, 15 days @ 52s 6d (£2.625)	£39 7s 6d	(£39.375)
1 Dec	Mr Fison, Conservative Agent. Hire of Humber car and driver to Parham, Marlesford, avoiding flooded roads.	15s 0d	(75p)

1911

11 June	Coronation Committee. Hire of Argyll and driver.	£1 10s 0d	(£1.50)
15 Aug	Duchess of Hamilton. Hire of Argyll car and driver for Kimbolton Castle. 4 days @ 3 guineas	£12 12s 0d	(£12.60)

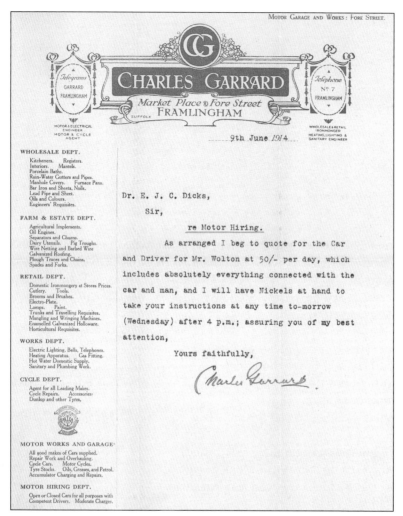

MOTOR GARAGE AND WORKS : FORE STREET.

Telegrams GARRARD FRAMLINGHAM

CHARLES GARRARD
Market Place & Fore Street
FRAMLINGHAM
SUFFOLK

Telephone N° 7 FRAMLINGHAM

MOTOR & ELECTRICAL ENGINEER MOTOR & CYCLE AGENT

WHOLESALE & RETAIL IRONMONGER HEATING, LIGHTING & SANITARY ENGINEER

9th June 1914

WHOLESALE DEPT.
Kitcheners. Registers.
Interiors. Mantels.
Porcelain Baths.
Rain-Water Gutters and Pipes.
Manhole Covers. Furnace Pans.
Bar Iron and Sheets, Nails.
Lead Pipe and Sheet.
Oils and Colours.
Engineers' Requisites.

FARM & ESTATE DEPT.
Agricultural Implements.
Oil Engines.
Separators and Churns.
Dairy Utensils. Pig Troughs.
Wire Netting and Barbed Wire
Galvanized Roofing.
Plough Traces and Chains.
Spades and Forks.

RETAIL DEPT.
Domestic Ironmongery at Stores Prices.
Cutlery. Tools.
Brooms and Brushes.
Electro-Plate.
Lamps. Paint.
Trunks and Travelling Requisites.
Mangling and Wringing Machines.
Enamelled Galvanized Holloware.
Horticultural Requisites.

WORKS DEPT.
Electric Lighting, Bells, Telephones.
Heating Apparatus. Gas Fitting.
Hot Water Domestic Supply.
Sanitary and Plumbing Work.

CYCLE DEPT.
Agent for all Leading Makes.
Cycle Repairs. Accessories.
Dunlop and other Tyres.

MOTOR WORKS AND GARAGE
All good makes of Cars supplied.
Repair Work and Overhauling.
Cycle Cars. Motor Cycles.
Tyre Stocks. Oils, Greases, and Petrol.
Accumulator Charging and Repairs.

MOTOR HIRING DEPT.
Open or Closed Cars for all purposes with
Competent Drivers. Moderate Charges.

Dr. E. J. C. Dicks,

    Sir,

        re Motor Hiring.

        As arranged I beg to quote for the Car
and Driver for Mr. Wolton at 50/- per day, which
includes absolutely everything connected with the
car and man, and I will have Nickels at hand to
take your instructions at any time to-morrow
(Wednesday) after 4 p.m.; assuring you of my best
attention,

    Yours faithfully,

    Charles Garrard

The hire of motor cars was only one part of Charles Garrard's business activities. An Argyll was extensively used, along with a Humber, a Darracq and a Model T Ford.

1912

16 March	Dr Drew. Hire of 12hp Humber and driver for professional visits.	10s 0d	(50p)
7 Oct	Board of Agriculture (Intelligence Division). Hire of Argyll car and driver.	£2 2s 0d	(£2.10)

1913

12 March	A. Macqueen, Framlingham College. Hire of touring car for Melton Golf Links.	17s 6d	(87.5p)
4 April	E. Suffolk County Council Public Health Dept. Hire of Darracq and driver for Medical Inspector.	10s 0d	(50p)

1914

4 Aug	Territorials, Captain Clarke.		
	Hire of car and driver.	£1 0s 0d	(£1.00)
26 June	P. Wolton.		
	Hire of Argyll car and driver for tour.		
	As quoted, 14 days @ 50s (£2.50)	£35 0s 0d	(£35.00)

1915

18 Jan	Northampton Field Artillery Regiment.		
	Journeys from Easton.	£1 3s 0d	(£1.15)
22 Jan	Public House Trust.		
	Hire of Ford and driver for Dennington		
	and Fressingfield.	10s 0d	(50p)
13 May	Archdeacon of Suffolk.		
	Hire of car and driver for Earl Soham.	4s 6d	(22.5p)
25 July	Sgt Hilling, Ammunition Column RFA.		
	Hire of Ford and driver for Marlesford.	10s 6d	(52.5p)

1916

4 April	2/3rd London Brigade RFA.		
	Hire of Ford and driver for Veterinary Officer		
	to Orford.	£1 0s 0d	(£1.00)

1917

28 June	P. Wolton.		
	Hire of landaulette for Diss Lamb Sale.	£1 14s 6d	(£1.725)
13 Aug	Business Expense.		
	Ford car to Ipswich for repairs to Argyll.	19s 0d	(95p)

1918

27 April	Duchess of Hamilton. Red Cross Account.		
	Hire of Argyll and driver for conveying wounded		
	from Campsey Ash station.*	14s 0d	(70p)
25 June	Rev Key, OTC.		
	Hire of landaulette and driver for College and		
	Kenton Station.	12s 6d	(62.5p)

1919

27 Feb	N. Lewis.		
	Hire of landaulette and driver to Earl Soham for		
	'Welcome Home Concert' at Assembly Hall.	15s 0d	(75p)

*The Marquis of Graham and Lady Mary Hamilton had turned their mansion at Easton Park into a Red Cross Hospital for the war wounded.

During the First World War, Olive Turney from Barsham near Beccles, moved to Ipswich in order to help with the war work. Fortunately for us she kept a diary relating to her time with Ransomes Sims & Jefferies, where her task was to drive a lorry with aeroplane parts from their White City works to the railway station. In addition, she also drove a taxi for Egertons. From her diary it is apparent that Olive came from a well-off family – she found that being with the 'poorer classes' gave her a better insight into their lives and was an experience she would never regret. The following extracts from her diary in 1917 relate to her taxi experiences.

I wouldn't have believed it possible that I could have so much enjoyed a life so totally different from what I had been accustomed to. But it was great fun – the freedom and unconventionality of it all, sitting in a taxi on a rank waiting for jobs, and all day long running about somewhere. I don't think there can possibly be a town [Ipswich] with worse streets for driving in than this. I don't mean the surface of them, which isn't bad on the whole, and where there is worse, the pavement is quite all right. But they are so narrow, and so many corners, and the traffic is regulated hardly at all.

Driving in a busy town where there is always a good deal of traffic is always more or less of a strain, particularly with streets such rabbit warrens as these, and one needs no extra anxieties thrown in. I think the people walking are the worst offenders. A very favourite trick is to step off the pavement right in front of your car when a tram is also meeting you at the same time. You are left a choice of swerving into the tram – when you get most decidedly the worst – or of running over the individual – which you most heartily wish you might, or of bringing the car to a standstill – which you do, invariably cursing. When you have jammed your brakes on hard, nearly jerking the people in the back of your car off the seat two or three times in one street only, and know that you must drive all the time expecting someone to step into the road without looking to see what is coming, you soon lose patience. Saturday is some day for me. I drive the lorry in the morning, in the afternoon a private car and then the taxi in the evening again, so there is a good variety and I have the two extremes of motor driving – the ultra respectable with the private car and then the low taxi. Well, there is more real amusement in the low taxi driving!! But I do really enjoy the driving on Saturday afternoons too. The car is a nice one, a Wolseley and she drives very well, and the ease and comfort of her after the lumbering lorry is very attractive. The people who own the car are rather amusing – a couple getting on in years, who very much dress the part. There is a good deal of motor veil and on cold days the man wears a fur cap of the peculiar breed with flaps which always reminds one of a polar bear. He is a good-sized man, and with a very benevolent manner, but he looks the last word in fierceness when in motor costume. We usually go to the seaside for the afternoons run, which I love. I really make an awfully good thing out of this Saturday afternoon stunt, as I get a jolly run in a good car, all the fun of the drive and the enjoyment of the country air and sea, and then am paid for doing it!!

Saturday evening is a huge contrast to the rest of the day. Even the car is getting on for the extreme contrast in size. A Ford landaulette feels the most awfully funny little tucked-up affair after a lorry and it's a good thing I go down

Olive Turney drove all manner of vehicles in the Ipswich area during the First World War, but reserved these comments for her Model T taxi: 'I think a Ford in any walk of life is incapable of real respectability, though I have the greatest admiration for them in many ways – but they are rattle traps.'

in size in easy stages. There certainly is no very marked air of respectability about a taxi. I think a Ford in any walk of life is incapable of real respectability though I have the greatest admiration for them in many ways – but they are rattle traps. Last Saturday was quite a typical busy evening. Little ghost jobs, for people catching trains or in a hurry to get to some place of amusement. Often one gets back on to the rank and doesn't even have time to shut off the engine before another fare rushes up. I like it like that. It's awfully dull sitting on the rank at night if it's not busy as you can't see the people the same as in the day. One has to be pretty smart getting fares on a Saturday and it's fatal to remain sitting in the car. The only thing is to stand in front – leaning against the radiator for warmth – and keep an eagle eye turned in all directions. Even then there are one or two men who seem to have a perfect genius for spotting fares coming even in the dark from ever so far off. This rank has no proper order of moving out, so the most jobs come to the quickest and there is a certain satisfaction in spotting a fare coming and stepping out, and almost personally conducting him to your car. I finished up on Saturday by taking a very drunk officer who had been run in by the APM back to his billet in a neighbouring town 8 miles off. The APM went too and a very smart sergeant major also, who sat in front with me. Having reached the town we then had to find this wretched man's billet, and so sorted out another officer from the HQ there to assist matters. We eventually found the place after some little time, and the drunk officer was safely stowed away, and

POTTER & WIGHTMAN

Motor and Cycle Engineers, Gas, Hot & Cold Water Fitters,

HIGH STREET, LEISTON.

MotorCars
(*Short or Long Journeys*)
On Hire.

CYCLES
Agents for ALL the best Makers.
A good stock to select from.

CYCLE ACCESSORIES.   **CYCLE REPAIRS.**

GUNS & AMMUNITION.   *All kinds of Cartridges stocked.*

New and Up-to-date Gas Fittings.   Estimates given for Installation and Repairs.   Mantles and Fittings of all kinds in stock.
Agent for Minimax Fire Extinguisher.

PROMPTNESS.   EFFICIENCY.   RELIABILITY.

POTTER and WIGHTMAN, LEISTON.

This 1913 advertisement is typical of a small firm which was not reliant on any one line of business, with hire work as a useful sideline.

then my wretched engine shut off and the sergeant major and I nearly hurt ourselves starting it again. Anyone who knows what an obstinate Ford can be like will appreciate my feelings. The sergeant major was rather friendly, he thought there ought to be a self starter in any car a woman drove, as 'no female ought to do much of that kind of work'.

The question of tips is an interesting one and I can quite see why the men like taxi-driving so much, apart from the independent life. We were told when first we began taxi driving that the tips made a very considerable addition to our wages, but we rather naturally thought that people would be sure to spot that we were only taxi drivers 'for the duration' and would consequently not add anything to the proper fare. But it's quite surprising. Lots of people very quickly realised that we were not doing this for a living, but they either tipped as a matter of course, or else suggested we bought chocolates or something of that kind. It was rather embarrassing at first, as we didn't like to refuse, but many of the fares were far more embarrassed than we, and in some cases apologised. Then of course there were the mean-minded who wouldn't have given any driver a tip, but made a point of trying to make you think it was because they had seen you were a lady!! I always used to average 30s a week, and have made more than £2, and even now can make quite a nice little sum on Saturday nights. I know some people thought we ought not to take tips. But why not? And it's not quite fair to the ones who are earning their living if one doesn't do as they do. People very soon get to know the drivers who would take them for less money, and that would have been jolly unfair to the men. Of course the men wangle most tremendously.

On a long run they think nothing of sticking on 10s or more and they never do a late job at night without ensuring a good bit for themselves. Well I don't blame them. I know what it's like now to be kept waiting on a cold night outside a dance or a card party – or to have a burst tyre on a country road miles from anywhere, at 12.30am and have to change a wheel by the uncertain light of an oil lamp. To be a taxi driver for a few months makes one learn to have a little consideration for the driver, and we have had an eye-opening education in many ways.

Although most motoring firms would have had a car available for private hire, there were few who dealt exclusively with this aspect of the trade. Vic Last was one of the first in Ipswich, and started his hire business from Crown Hall Garage in Crown Street. As the son of a farmer who operated several teams of threshing tackle, he had been sent to Coventry to learn the steam business. On his return, though, he decided to pursue his own ideas, and moved to No 23 High Street, Ipswich, in about 1914. He applied to the Council for hackney carriage plates, which allowed him to ply for hire on the Cornhill, amongst the horse cabs.

William Clarke was still using this photograph for his advertisements in 1922, whereas the Unic hire cars are from a pre-war period. An important detail is the circular 10mph speed limit sign. This lower limit could be adopted by the Local Government Board if a suitable case for it could be proven.

MOTOR GARAGE,

BEACH ROAD EAST, FELIXSTOWE.

UP-TO-DATE TAXI CABS. TOURING CARS. MOTOR CHAR-A-BANC FOR HIRE.

W. G. CLARKE, Motor Engineer,

'Whippet' Chenery obtained his licence to operate a taxi when he was about 18 years old, just after the First World War. During his working life he drove an interesting variety of cars, including this left-hand drive Buick on the rank in Lloyds Avenue, Ipswich, c. 1934.

Another early taxi driver was William Chenery, or 'Whippet' as he was invariably called. His father had been a horse cab proprieter in Felixstowe, but the business suffered badly in the war as many of his horses were requisitioned. The family moved to Ipswich, when Whippet's father bought him his first car, a Napier. At the age of 18, just after the war, he also started to work from the Cornhill, with other drivers such as Ernie Andews (Unic), G. Baxter (Sharon), Bill Button (Talbot), and Bill Cook (Napier). Whippet remained a taxi driver for most of his working life, with an interesting range of cars, from Minerva to Buick, Packard and Ford Pilot. He found the work enjoyable and would often make very long journeys that other drivers declined. Being a sole operator he would take all the work that came along, which frequently meant a seven-day working week.

Vic Last's business barely survived the war before it folded, and the family moved to Woodbridge Road, where he was able to start again, hiring an old Maltings nearby. After a while he had acquired about six cars and one or two drivers in addition to himself, and trade was improving.

However, one morning, on reaching the garages he found that children had broken in and wrecked two of his cars. The glass and instruments were smashed, dirt had been put in the sumps, and the damage was such that they were virtually written off. Although two of the children were caught, their parents were out of work and there was no prospect of recovering any money. It took Vic a long time to recover from this great loss. Vandalism is nothing new.

One of the cars he had bought secondhand was a Renault, described by the vendor as follows:

> 12/16hp Renault, four-cylinder, magneto, three speeds and reverse, blue paint unscratched, upholstered Bedford cloth, three back and two folding seats inside, one beside driver in front, luggage rail, roof lamp, Stepney, five lamps, price £450. Specially suited for hire work, fast, economical on petrol and oil.

Among Vic's regular clients during this period were the Ord sisters. Every year they would employ him to take them on holiday, usually touring throughout Wales or Scotland or the area of their choice. This made a pleasant change from the normal run of work.

Vic Last started his hire business from Crown Street in Ipswich. His first car was a 12/16hp Renault, which was very popular with wedding parties. Note the dashboard-mounted radiator.

Although road conditions had improved by the 1920s, the country areas still had many dirt roads, with stones being used to fill in the worst craters. The main roads and most of those in Ipswich were tarred, but in some areas around the town centre the surface was treacherous. It consisted of flat wooden blocks which would swell when wet, offering a very uneven slippery surface. Vic's son Clifford discovered this the hard way when he was deposited, along with his motorcycle, under a trolley bus, with painful results.

By the early 1930s, Vic had moved his business and family to a large fourteen-room house in Christchurch Street. Several of these rooms were let to guests, many of whom were stars performing at the local Hippodrome. Christchurch Street Garage was built to house at least half a dozen cars, and had a pit and servicing facilities. By this time Vic was concentrating on private hire, and his business flourished for several years until ill health forced him into early retirement.

Although car ownership now is relatively cheaper than ever, there will always be a need for hire cars. Many country areas do not have an adequate public transport service and in towns, parking, vandalism and congestion can make car ownership questionable. The hire car provides a solution to these problems.

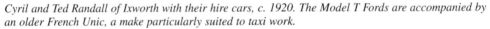

Cyril and Ted Randall of Ixworth with their hire cars, c. 1920. The Model T Fords are accompanied by an older French Unic, a make particularly suited to taxi work.

CHAPTER EIGHT

MOTORCYCLING

It is a sad fact that many people today are prejudiced against motorcycles, for a variety of reasons. For those who have enjoyed the pleasures of motorcycling, the memories remain, and most would wish to recapture them if possible.

At the beginning of the century, the social attitude towards motorcycling was completely different. For example, the Anglian Motor Co claimed that several prominent gentlemen in the neighbourhood had their motorcycles in constant use, and the President of the Bury St Edmunds Motorcycle Club in 1915 was The Honourable Walter Guinness MP.

A typical garage may have developed from a cycle shop, becoming involved with the sale or repair of cars and motorcycles. The numbers for both were so small at that time that little thought was given to dealing exclusively with either two or four wheels; after all, they both had an engine and were exploiting this marvellous new form of transport. Although the Motor Car Act of 1903 required all drivers to have a licence, the lower age limit for a motorcycle was only 14.

From the Ipswich vehicle registrations of 1904, it is clear that motorcycles and tricars outnumbered motor cars. This was not just a local effect as the figures for the whole of England over the first eighteen months of registration, show nearly 53 per cent of vehicles were motorcycles. In subsequent years the motor car started to take a greater share of sales, although this trend was reversed during the First World War.

Ipswich Borough Council – Ratio of Vehicles Registered		
	Motor Cars %	Motorcycles %
1904	49	51
1905	47	53
1906	62	38
1907	76	24

In common with motorcyclists, early motorists were also exposed to the elements. Before the 1920s most cars were of the open type, with the occupants having to be well dressed to protect themselves from bad weather. However, with the advent of the closed car, they were then able to arrive smartly dressed at their destination. The car

The Anglian Cycle & Engineering Co Ltd of Stowmarket produced this Clement-powered motorcycle in 1903 – which is still in use today. The development of such machines from the bicycle is clearly evident.

also cost more than the motorcycle and appeared to be safer. Many years later, minority elements gained bad publicity for motorcycling, and these factors all combined to generate a large void between the general acceptability of cars and motorcycles. The image seems to have improved in recent years, but unfortunately the old British motorcycle industry is not around to take advantage of it.

Returning to the early years, motorcycle development was actively pursued, as fitting an engine into a cycle frame was a logical move and easy to accomplish. Motorised tricycles were popular, with De Dion engines being extensively used at the end of the last century.

One of the earliest motorcycles in Suffolk was owned by Frank Burrell of Fornham St Martin. He bought a 1.25hp Belgian-made Minerva in 1899. This machine had a surface carburettor which relied on an induction pipe from the air space above the petrol in the tank. One day, when riding through Lavenham, there was a great explosion from his motorcycle – not unusual with this induction layout. It caused great excitement, with many of the women leaving their looms and rushing into the street to see what had happened.

Frank also entered one of the first recorded motorcycle competition events, a five-mile handicap race on the cricket meadow in Cemetery Road, Bury St Edmunds, organised by the Bicycle and Athletic Club in 1902. The *Bury Free Press* reported:

> The five-mile motorcycle handicap was one of the most attractive events of the afternoon, and it is gratifying to be able to record that the fears of some of the officials as to accidents were not realised. In fact the manner in which the 'motorists' managed to steer their machines was an admirable demonstration of the amount of control which their riders possessed over them. The only mishap was when Mr T. H. Nice skidded after he had done several laps. Up to this point he was doing splendidly, and was continually cheered by the spectators; in fact had it not been for this untoward incident, there is little doubt that it would have been his race. A silver cup was presented to H. Harper for first place by the Marquess of Bristol, and Frank Burrell came second.

It should be remembered that with a speed limit of initially 12 and then 20mph, there was little incentive to build high-speed motorcycles, and the engine was mainly seen as a useful means of getting up hills. The early machines were developed as motorised bicycles, still retaining their pedals. They did not have the benefit of a clutch or gears, so any obstruction in the road would mean stopping the engine.

The following Suffolk firms were involved with the production of motorcycles, sidecars and various three-wheeled devices. The first two have already been mentioned under motor car manufacture.

Anglian Cycle & Engineering Co Ltd, Anglian Works, Stowmarket

This firm seems to have been more active in the production of motorcycles than cars. Although few written details remain, it is fortunate indeed that a 1903 model still exists, and has been restored by Don French. It has a Clement engine with automatic intake valve, bicycle-type handlebars with stirrup front brake, and rear brake onto the belt drive rim. There are two main controls, fitted either side of the petrol tank, the right hand one being a throttle, the other a combined exhaust lifter and ignition advance and retard. There is no clutch.

Don kindly allowed the author to ride his Anglian.

> I sat on the saddle, feeling distinctly uneasy about the absence of a clutch, and peddled off, desperately trying to remember which position the levers should be in. After a few gyrations of the pedals the valve lift lever was dropped, and the engine burst into life. There was a sensation of the crankshaft being directly coupled to the back wheel, as the individual firing impulses pushed me forward, although the belt drive does provide considerable shock absorption. After a while I could appreciate Don's advice – to simply drive the Anglian on the throttle lever. The difficulty occurs when you need to slow right down, as the engine loses all power yet is still connected to the rear wheel. With judicious use of the pedals, I was able to negotiate a sharp right angle bend, reinstate the power, and thankfully be on the straight again. I must admit to enjoying the ride on a bright summer's day on a fairly straight private road, but can well imagine the difficulties with larger engined bikes in a wet town centre.

The firm continued as Stannard & Co, but it is not clear when motorcycle production ceased.

Anglian Motor Co Ltd, Station Road and Newgate Street, Beccles

William Robinson's earliest work was with bicycles; the production of motor cycles was an obvious step and was to outlive production of the company's own cars. Prior to the formation of the Anglian Motor Company Ltd, Robinson had produced his own Clifton motorcycles, which were powered by De Dion engines. By way of variation, a trailer could also be towed, or a forecar was available. This additional flexibility was important as it allowed the motorcycle to be used for a wider range of tasks.

Towards the end of 1903 the new company was selling Anglian motorcycles from £45. Three machines were shown at the Crystal Palace Show that year, each with 2.75hp De Dion engines, one of them water cooled. The models were designated No 1 and No 2, the latter a lower priced and lighter version of No 1.

At least two Beccles Anglians have survived, one of these being a very tall 1903 machine now belonging to John Moore. He bought it in derelict condition from a member of the Saunderson family in the 1950s. Its original registration is AM292, ie Anglian Motor 292 cc, which must be one of the earliest personalised number plates.

The 'Trimo' was an Anglian three-wheeled device that claimed to take two passengers up the steepest of hills without assistance. It could also be had with 'free engine' option to permit the rider to mount before starting, a useful device in those days before the clutch became commonplace.

1904 saw much publicity for the company – they had full-page advertisements in *The Motor*, and the well-known rider of the day, H. J. Densham, became the first person to take any mechanical vehicle up 'Steep Hill' in Lincoln, a feat previously considered impossible. His 2.75hp No 1 Anglian climbed the hill with ease on three occasions. Machines were exhibited at the Stanley Show that year, where the lightweight model was fitted with a 2.5hp JAP engine.

The performance of early motorcycles was limited by the single-gear direct-drive arrangement in general use. By 1905 the Anglian Motor Co Ltd had patented their own two-speed gear, with a conversion available for fitting to any make of motorcycle, at a cost of £10–£12. It was particularly aimed at motorcyclists who wished to convert their machines to tricars.

The female motorist was not forgotten: in the same year a new tricar was produced that could be driven by ladies, with no crossbar or petrol tank to straddle. It was powered by two 5hp air-cooled engines, transmitting power through the new two-speed transmission. The forecarriage was coachbuilt and provided with footboards.

The Anglian Motor Co Ltd of Beccles manufactured a range of two- and three-wheeled vehicles. For 1908 they included this tricar with water-cooled 3.5hp De Dion engine. Transmission choices for their motorcycles varied between their own two-speed drive, or an 8-foot long Shamrock Gloria leather belt, which assured 'perfect drive without undue strain on the bearings'.

The company's 1908 catalogue offered the following machines:

Light Tricar	3.5hp De Dion engine	£65 10s 0d (£65.50)
Two-Speed Tourist Motorcycle	2.75hp De Dion engine, weight 160lbs	£50 0s 0d
No 1 Model	2.75hp De Dion engine, weight 140lbs	£36 0s 0d
No 2 Model	2.5hp JAP engine, weight 93lbs	£26 0s 0d

From an advert in the 1913 *Suffolk County Handbook*, it appears that the company name had reverted to William Robinson, although he was still the sole manufacturer of Anglian Motor bicycles and two-speed gears.

Lion Cycle Company, 267 London Road South, Lowestoft

As early as 1900, this company was receiving coverage in the motoring press. Their main product was a motorcycle that could be converted to a tandem tricycle in about five minutes by removing the front wheel and replacing it with a forecarriage. Powered by a 2.25hp De Dion engine, the transmission was all-chain drive via an intermediate countershaft to provide a reduction ratio. Unlike most machines of the time, it was not fitted with pedals, and could reach a claimed 40mph in solo form.

By 1903, a refinement of the tandem was being offered, with an upholstered forecarriage on C springs. In addition, there was a further seat in front for a child of three to six years old, with a dummy steering wheel to keep him – or her –amused. The implications of an accident with such a vehicle do not bear contemplating. It is interesting to note that the 1903 machine had adopted the more conventional belt drive rather than the earlier all-chain transmission.

William Montgomery, Brentgovel Street, Bury St Edmunds

Many manufacturers were experimenting with methods for carrying an additional passenger on a motorcycle, with tricars, tandems, trailers, detachable forecars and all manner of weird devices being tried. However, it was the sidecar that was to eventually eclipse all other methods, and in 1903 William Montgomery was manufacturing and selling ten different models throughout the country.

At a time when other people were producing rigid chairs, Montgomery was enjoying success with his 'flexible' sidecar. The compensating joints allowed the motorcycle to lean over in the normal way, and it was claimed that a corner could be taken at any speed possible with a solo! However, the motorcycle writer Ixion was not over impressed.

> Maybe I handled my Montgomery chairs rather too roughly, but sooner or later they always shifted their attachments on the bicycle frame, with lamentable effects on the steering. Moreover, they could behave oddly on steep cambers, when the chair might lean in against the bicycle, and nip my corpulent thighs most painfully.

Montgomery sidecars were manufactured in Bury St Edmunds before the First World War and sold throughout the country. William Montgomery is accompanied here by R.C. Marsh in the sidecar, at Hawkedon Hall, c. 1904. The firm moved to Coventry and became well known for their own motorcycles during the 1920s and '30s.

At the 1903 Crystal Palace Show, the following were exhibited:

> Six side carriages, fitted with best-quality cane bodies, plated rims, Dunlop tyres, upholstered in leather, with apron. Price £12 10s 0d (£12.50).
> Four side carriages, similar to above, but selling for £10 10s 0d (£10.50.)
> Two 'Ensign' Modele de Luxe Motor Bicycles, with 2.75hp engines, finished in black enamel and lined in gold. Price 45 guineas (£47.25).

Don French is also the owner of a Bury St Edmunds-built two-speed Montgomery Ensign, powered by a Stevens engine. This is probably the only Bury-built machine still existing.

One particular novelty consisted of a motorcycle with a sidecar fixed to each side. Also, a 688cc machine, powered by a horizontally opposed twin-cylinder engine of their own manufacture, caused great excitement in the motorcycling press when announced in 1913, selling for the sum of £80 15s 0d (£80.75). By this time, though, the company had moved to Coventry, where they went on to produce a wide range of machines with Villiers, Anzani and JAP engines. They also produced the first frames and front forks for the Brough Superior motorcycles, and continued in business until the beginning of the Second World War. The Bury St Edmunds connection was maintained for a number of years, as they were still advertising 'Ensign' bicycles from No 6 Brentgovel Street in 1916.

Prospective motorcyclists could buy a standard machine, such as the Ariel, from the Ipswich ironmongery firm of Martin & Newby. Mr Newby himself registered an Ariel, No DX13, in 1904, and continued to sell the make for a number of years.

Alternatively, it was common for a firm to put their own name on a motorcycle that they were selling. Alfred Adams in Woodbridge was offering his 'St John' motorcycle in 1903, and BJ78 is registered as such. They were powered by a Brown engine, and that particular firm also manufactured complete motorcycles. The 'St John' element of it was probably 'badge engineering'. Another example was the Ipswich metal-plating firm of Kenyon & Trott who sold a number of 'K & T' machines around 1904, based on the Clement Garrard motorcycle.

Registration records also show that a number of individual machines were produced by enthusiasts, but these are unlikely to have been part of any serious attempt at quantity production.

The 1904 DX records show that 88 per cent of registered motorcycles were manufactured in England, by twenty-two separate companies. This is in complete contrast with registered motor cars for the same year, where 80 per cent were manufactured by three French companies.

The Egerton family were, of course, involved with motorcycles from the beginning. In September 1899 Hubert drove his 2.25hp De Dion tricycle from Land's End to Norwich in two days, and in 1901 became the first person to ride a motorcycle from Land's End to John O'Groats.

George Burton of Wherstead Park near Ipswich, with his wife on their Indian Vee twin, the archetypal American motorcycle. George was a keen motorcyclist, having owned a Triumph TT Roadster and a Douglas. Like so many young men, he was killed in the First World War.

His brother Reggie had a BAT motorcycle, one of the first machines to be produced without pedal assistance. It also had a sprung subframe and was considered as a fast racing motorcycle of its time. The lack of pedals was quite a novelty. When someone asked him what he would do if it broke down, Reggie replied in astonishment that he would use his brains to get him home, not his brawn!

On this machine, with its De Dion engine, he competed in the first organised motorcycle race to be held at Portman Road in Ipswich. The Suffolk County Championships Race Meeting was held in July 1904, and was promoted by the local athletic club. The track was normally used for athletics and cycle racing, and the motorcycle race was by way of an experiment, with two heats and a final over a distance of three miles.

In the first heat was T.H. Tessier of the BAT company, on one of his own machines. Unfortunately, his lack of pedals meant that he was lapped twice before he could get going properly. The heat was won by F. Barker on a Dart, in a time of 6 minutes 2.2 seconds, with an average speed of just under 30mph, but the crowd showed great sympathy with Tessier's efforts. The second heat had local man Reggie Egerton, W. Hodgkinson from Tottenham on a JAP (J.A. Prestwich machines built in Tottenham), and E. Fitzherbert of Lowestoft on a Belgian FN. The main battle was between Egerton and Hodgkinson, but Reggie started to flag after having made a good start. Hodgkinson appeared to gain impetus by jerking his body violently forward, and just

The first motorcycle race to be held in Ipswich was during an athletics meeting at Portman Road in 1904. The final race was over a distance of three miles, and won in a time of 5 minutes 54 seconds. BAT motorcycles were entered in these events, but were initially at a disadvantage as they were not fitted with pedals.

Frank, Arthur, Val and Leslie Revett on their Rudge-Whitworth motorcycles. Frank's machine is a later model with the saddle tank introduced in 1927. Rim-mounted brakes are evident on the two older bikes. Note the posters for the Air Pageant at Hadleigh aerodrome.

managed to beat Egerton by half a wheel. The heat itself was won by over 80 yards by Fitzherbert. The final was won by Barker, who managed to improve his time to 5 minutes 54.2 seconds.

The introduction of motorcycle races into athletic and cycle meetings was to become popular. In Southwold, for example, the annual athletic sports meeting held two- and three-mile motorcycle races in the years around 1911.

W.D. Chitty, who has already been mentioned in connection with Botwoods Ltd, was a very enthusiastic motorcyclist in his younger days. Between 1907 and 1912 he had considerable success on tracks such as Brooklands, Crystal Palace, White City, Canning Town, Birmingham, Cambridge and Paris. In 1909–10 he broke a number of track and world records, including the one-hour championship cup at Brooklands.

One of the earliest people to specialise in the sale of bicycles and motorcycles was Charles Hammond, whose original premises were at 6–8 St Nicholas Street in Ipswich. He produced his own bicycle, called the 'Gainsborough', and then proceeded to build motorcycles and tricars using the same name. His brother-in-law Valentine Revett came to work for him in 1905. Two years later Val started his own cycle business with limited capital at No 1 Berners Street. During the week, he would borrow his brother-in-law's best bicycle so that he could display it in the window of his own shop. From these small beginnings, the Revett family and business expanded until they had eleven children and the name Revett became synonymous with motorcycles throughout East Anglia.

This delightful photograph from the late 1920s is of Bill Driver on his 1926 3.5hp Triumph, with Bert Pryke in the foreground on a 1923 Villiers-powered 2-stroke Carfield. Both men were from Bramfield. Carfield motorcycles were made between 1919 and 1924. The Triumph was destroyed by fire in 1930.

In 1912 Val opened another cycle shop in St Matthews Street, and during this period started working on motorcycles as well. He went off to war in 1914, assuring his wife that it would all be over in two weeks. Needless to say, she was to become very conversant with the sale and repair of bicycles over the next four years.

On his return, Val made a positive move into motorcycles, and by 1921 had acquired a shop in Granville Street for that purpose. He gained the agency for Rudge motorcycles and over the years many of the well-known British makes followed, including AJS, Matchless, Norton, Francis Barnett, James, and BSA.

Berners Street was expanded to take in No 3, and a new garage built for a showroom and repairs in the orchard at the rear of Holton Hall dairy on Barrack Corner. In 1932 an even finer showroom was opened at 67 St Matthews Street, but a disastrous fire six years later destroyed nearly all the stock.

Val's son Geoff entered the family business in 1934, and was a very enthusiastic motorcyclist. His first machine, an Alldays, was bought for 10s (50p) and pushed to Akenham, where he tried it out round a farmer's field. This was a common introduction to the motorcycle for many who live in the country, and the author clearly recalls his first ride on Brian Martin's 350cc Ariel around a field in Monewden. The open exhaust and the smell of the grass and oil on the Red Hunter engine are not easily forgotten.

In the 1920s Geoff visited the Speed Trials at Shrubland Park near Ipswich, where timed sprints were held over the narrow drive leading up to the house. These popular events for cars and motorcycles were in aid of the Ipswich and East Suffolk Hospital, and several well-known works riders competed. The 1927–8 races were recorded on cine film, and a copy is held by the East Anglian Film Archive at the University of East Anglia in Norwich.

Geoff naturally competed in various sporting activities, generally using the same machine but with modifications to tyres and handlebars, etc. Although his favourite machine for trials was the Ariel, a 500cc Triumph Tiger 100 with special bronze cylinder head was used for scrambles, road racing and general road use. Geoff competed at Donnington Park on several occasions, and at the famous Brooklands track prior to its closure in 1939.

After the First World War there was a long period before normal sporting activities resumed. It was not until 1921 that the Ipswich and District Motor Cycle Club organised its first competition, a Hill Climb at Battisford. Fastest time of the day (FTD) went to R. Fenn on his 3.5hp Triumph, who recorded 15 seconds over the 300-yard course, with a flying start. Fenn was without doubt the local ace, and had been winning races since before the war, invariably Triumph mounted. The Club was very involved in sporting events and the following is a brief selection of typical activities over the ensuing years:

1921   Flying-kilometre races timed on section of straight road at East Bergholt. The electric timing failed and they had to revert to a system of flags.

Reuben Bryanton outside his Witnesham garage in the 1920s. His sign states that he is a motorcycle and cycle engineer. He would have provided a useful service in the area, particularly as the garage had a Bowser petrol pump.

Reliability trial. This type of event was very popular, and this one started at the Sproughton Wild Man, via Burstall water splash, Bullen Wood, Bramford Tye, Flowton Church, Somersham, Burstall, Elmsett, Aldham, Hadleigh, and back to Sproughton. Riders were required to maintain 20mph over the course of approximately 30 miles.

1923 Hill Climb at Cooks Hill, Manningtree, with pneumatic timing system. Fenn again made FTD, but it was noted that a considerable amount of traffic interfered with the proceedings. This was a regular venue of the time.

1924 Hill Climb at Belstead Brook Hill, a 1 in 10 gradient with two difficult bends. Electric timing still gave FTD to Fenn.

1925 Beach racing at Sizewell. Over 2,000 people attended the racing, which took place over a half-mile course.
Shrubland Park Speed Trials on a 1.3-mile course from the Russian Lodge Gate. Ernie Searle on a Norton takes FTD for a change.

1927 Motor Cycle Gymkhana at Euston Park.
Speed trials held at Kesgrave Hall fete.

The Ipswich Club was also involved with helping local children. For its second outing in 1923, over 400 poor children were taken to Little Glemham Park for the day. This form of charity outing was to be a regular event over the years.

Rattlesden Hill Climb, 1924. Charlie Claxton gives a spirited ride in the sidecar class. Crash helmets and crowd safety measures were clearly not of much importance then.

Shrubland Park Speed Trials, near Ipswich, 1926. Local rider Fenn (Triumph), and Ernie Searle (Norton), crouch down for maximum speed at this popular event.

The opening of the new concrete sea wall at north Lowestoft was to have other uses apart from keeping the elements at bay. It was soon realised that the new facility would make an excellent race track and provide good publicity for the town. Following initial speed trials in 1926, the first major races were held the next year, when it was estimated that the crowd of spectators approached 20,000. Racing took place over one kilometre from a standing start, with a further 1,000 yards for stopping. The track allowed two competitors to race against each other, separated by a blue line painted on the ground. An electronic timing system enabled the elapsed times and handicap penalties to be determined with accuracy.

The 1927 Lowestoft races were primarily for motorcycles, and were organised by the Ipswich Club. They attracted many well-known names of the period, such as Barry Baragwanath (996cc Brough Superior), Ernie Searle (Norton) and Ian Riddoch (Zenith Blackburne). There were many different classes of racing, with the following main results.

Solo up to 250cc	E. Harvey (Ipswich)	Harvey Special	34.3 sec
Solo up to 350cc	F. Neill (Ipswich)	Matchless	33.2 sec
Solo up to 500cc	E. Searle (Bury St Edmunds)	Norton	29.0 sec
Solo up to 750cc	E. Searle	588cc Norton	27.0 sec
Solo up to 1000cc	I. Riddoch (Ipswich)	988cc Zenith	27.2 sec
	E. Searle	588cc Norton	27.2 sec

The start line at the Kesgrave Speed Trials, held at the Hall around 1927.

The 1,000cc run-off was won by Ernie Searle, as the Zenith Blackburne was unable to get away.   He could obviously do no wrong at the meeting, and also put up the fastest time of 31 seconds for the 1,000cc sidecar event, outclassing Baragwanath who could only manage 37 seconds.

The races proved very popular, and in 1928 the Lowestoft and District Motor Club organised two events in conjunction with the Essex Motor Club, putting a greater emphasis on cars. It is interesting to note that the fastest car at the September meeting was a 1496cc Bugatti entered by W. D. Chitty and driven by his son Ron, with a time of 46.8 seconds.

Car and motorcycle enthusiasts often have strong views on their own favourite machinery, so the idea of a match race between fastest car and motorcycle caused great excitement. J. Storey had set the quickest time of 31.6 seconds on his 976cc Brough Superior, and therefore had to suffer a 15-second handicap. In the race, the big Vee twin was soon catching up the Bugatti, and overtook it just before the finishing line to win by 0.2 seconds.

During the inter-war years, there were several motorcycle clubs in Suffolk, whereas before then it was mainly limited to the Ipswich & District Motorcycle Club and the Bury and West Suffolk Clubs.

The following MCCs were active for varying periods in the 1920s and '30s, although there would have been other smaller clubs as well.

Beyton and District MCC
Bury St Edmunds and District MCC
Crane Ltd MCC
Ipswich and District MCC
Ipswich Red Triangle MCC
Leiston Works and District MCC
Lowestoft MCC
Stowmarket MCC
Sudbury MCC

In 1930, for example, the Beyton and District Motor Cycle Club organised their first grass track meeting, which was held near the church in Ixworth and described as the 'Ixworth Super Speedway'. The 'American' Hill Climbs at Mumbery Hills, Westleton, were held by the Leiston Club. Unlike earlier events – over a steep hill on a public road – this was on an approximate 1 in 3 gradient of sand and heather, near the coast. In 1937, A. Hare and Graham Kirk broke the record in 6.4 seconds, the former riding a 1,000cc Ariel. Geoff Revett won the 350cc class in 7 seconds on his Ariel. The next year saw the standard tyre prize being taken by A. Relle on his 980cc Brough Superior, in 6.8 seconds.

The Ipswich Red Triangle Club was founded in 1925 by a group of enthusiasts who met in the YMCA hut at Nacton. They felt there was a need for another club in the Ipswich area and named it after the symbol of the YMCA, which was not appreciated

A splendid photograph of the Ipswich and District Motorcycle Club outside the Running Buck on St Margarets Plain. Female members are confined to the sidecars, apart from one cheerful solo rider. The painted sign for Reggie Egerton's garage still exists in this location, although in a different form.

Len Corder, a prominent member of the Ipswich Red Triangle Club, with his Sunbeam-based special and collection of trophies.

by that organisation. The president and chairman in the early years were Major Everett and Val Revett respectively.

Speedway meetings were held in 1935 by the Lowestoft Club on their new track at Pakefield. Professional teams, consisting of six riders, competed in these races, averaging about 40mph over four laps. 'Squib Burton' from the Hackney Wick speedway team described the track as the finest of its kind he had ever seen.

The Colchester Castle Motorcycle Club held hill climb events at Polstead before the last war. Len Millbank on the Velocette is struggling to catch the Norton. Specialist riding gear had not progressed much over the years, and 'plus fours' and everyday clothing are still apparent.

Tornado Smith from Boxford was one of the country's greatest exponents on the Wall of Death, and spent most of his working life at the Southend Kursaal. On the limit here, the sidecar wheel is nudging the safety wire at the top of the Wall.

Outside the mainstream of motorcycle sport, lies the lesser known activity of Wall of Death riding. Today, Alan Ford is the sole operator of a Wall. In the 1930s, though, it was a popular spectacle at fairgrounds and seaside resorts throughout the country, and the leading exponent was a Suffolk man, George Smith from Boxford.

Having seen a Wall of Death ride as a young man, he decided that his future lay in that direction, and he soon gained experience working on the Wall at Whitly Bay before appearing regularly at the Kursaal in Southend.

The seasonal nature of his work meant that the winter period was spent in Boxford, where he was a skilled carpenter. Some relief was gained by a regular appearance in the Bertram Mills Christmas show at Olympia, where he met the young girl who was to become his wife and partner in all senses of the word. They started a double-act in 1931 under the names of Tornado Smith and Dynamite Doris, although she subsequently changed hers to Marjorie Dare.

Tornado was a great showman and always tried to incorporate a new act each year. His most famous stunt was the introduction of a lion cub, which initially crouched on the petrol tank but eventually resided in a sidecar when it grew too large. Another dangerous act was the first ascent of a Wall in this country using a car – an Austin Seven – for which feat he received a letter of congratulation from Sir Malcom Campbell. These daredevil exploits were hardly matched by his appearance, which usually consisted of riding boots, trousers, white shirt and tie, topped off with tortoiseshell glasses and a beret.

Tornado Smith's wife, who initially called herself 'Dynamite Doris', also rode the Wall on her Indian Scout. A fall during a show could have serious consequences. In this case she is fortunate to be nursing only an injured arm.

During the 1935 winter period, the Wall was dismantled at Southend and taken to Boxford for its annual maintenance. Tornado took the opportunity of demonstrating his skills and set up the Wall in the yard of The White Hart, where his parents were the landlords. People from miles around flocked to Boxford to see the five daily sessions, performed by Tornado and Marjorie Dare as they hurtled around the Wall on their Indian Vee twins. He then moved the Wall onto the Market Hill in Sudbury, where further performances raised £20 which was donated to the British Legion.

There is insufficient space here to tell the amazing story of Tornado Smith, but he did stay with The Wall of Death all his working life, and was still riding at Southend in the early 1960s.

Road racing seems almost sedate by comparison, but this has always been the zenith of motorcycle sport. As there were no road circuits in East Anglia before the Second World War, you needed to be very keen to compete regularly. One such person was Harley Deschamps who worked for Mann Egerton in Norwich, and later Botwoods in Ipswich. His first racer was a KTT Velocette, on which he competed at Donnington and Brooklands many times, but the bike covered a far greater number of miles on the local roads as his personal transport. Nowadays, motorcycles are very specialised, but originally one machine would often be used by a rider for all types of events, and be ridden to the track as well.

At the end of 1938, Harley traded in his current machine, a secondhand Norton, for a brand new 350 Manx Model. Most engineering firms were rapidly moving over to war work, and the new bike did not arrive until about a week before the Isle of Man races. Unfortunately, a damp road surface caused him and the Norton to part company on the second lap at Quarry Bend, resulting in a broken collar bone for him and somewhat more damage to the machine. The Norton went back for repair but, with the outbreak of war, Harley was unable to keep up the payments and was not to see it again until 1981, when he was reunited with it in the Isle of Man after being contacted by its present owner. Despite being paralysed, John Flood has carried out a full restoration of the Norton after acquiring it as a collection of parts in several cardboard boxes.

The period between the wars saw many changes in the design of motorcycles. Acetylene lamps, for example, were to be replaced by electric lighting, although this was often fitted only as an extra. Ignition was predominantly by magneto, and was to remain so until the late 1950s.

The motive power was usually a single-cylinder engine for capacities up to 500cc, and above that, the Vee twin. Side-valve designs were to be replaced by overhead valves, while two-strokes catered for the lower end of the capacity range.

Harley Deschamps with his new 350cc Manx Norton, prior to the start of the 1939 TT in the Isle of Man. Unfortunately a damp section of track was to see them part company on the second lap.

In the early 1920s some machines were still fitted with belt final drive, and hand-change gearboxes were standard. By the end of the decade, gear changing was being transferred to foot operation. There were few changes in the frame department, as girder forks and rigid rear end remained the standard throughout the period. A significant visual change was the replacement of the flat tank by the saddle tank, with varying degrees of colour and chrome plate.

By 1933 motorcycles were taxed by engine size rather than weight. The following rates were introduced:

Capacity Limit	Tax
150cc	15s (75p)
250cc	£1 10s 0d (£1.50)
over 250cc	£3

The above is a very broad comment on motorcycle development. There are many examples which do not fit the pattern and this, of course, makes it all the more interesting. Scott produced large-capacity water-cooled two-strokes, while in 1931 Ariel introduced their 500cc air-cooled four-cylinder model. Edward Turner's 498cc Triumph Speed Twin, which appeared in 1937, was to be the basis for so many of their well-known models in the post-war period.

The author's interest in motorcycling was heightened by the sight and sound of pre-unit Triumphs, mainly Tiger 100s, 110s and the occasional Norton. Exotic machinery such as the Gold Star BSA and Vincents were rarely seen, or affordable. Customised parallel twins were the preferred choice of most young motorcyclists, being decidedly sportier than the standard touring singles of the day. The rapid growth of the classic motorcycle scene in the late 1980s saw the value of British motorcycles rise to unbelievable heights. It is good that these old motorcycles will no longer be broken up, but sad if they become investments rather than machines to be ridden.

APPENDICES

APPENDIX A

The First Motor Car and Motorcycle Registrations
Issued by the County Borough of Ipswich, from January 1904

Registration	Make	Owner and Address
DX1	20hp Mercedes	W. Pretty, Chandos House, Fonnereau Road
DX2	3.5hp Quadricycle	E. Sayer, Warrington Road
DX3	10hp Renault	J. Pipe, 1 Corn Hill
DX4	10hp Georges Richard	H. Kettle, 24 Lower Brook Street
DX5	7hp Primus	G. Ching, 12 Warrington Road
DX6	6hp De Dion	C. K. Moseley, 14 Northgate Street
DX7	BAT motorcycle	L. Vulliamy, 12 Northgate Street
DX8	Ormonde motorcycle	N. Adlard, 15 Westerfield Road
DX9	Crypt tricycle	W. Ellengar, 47 Croft Street
DX10	Excelsior motorcycle	J. Daniels, 6 Norwich Road
DX11	8hp De Dion	Botwood & Egerton, Carr Street
DX12	5.5hp Peugeot	E. Rowe, Borough Asylum
DX13	Ariel motorcycle	A. Newby, 9 Warwick Road
DX14	12hp Gobron Brillié	Botwood & Egerton
DX15	4.5hp De Dion Bouton	J. Schilling, River View, New Cut
DX16	10hp Argyll	W. Burton, Edgehill, Stone Lodge Lane
DX17	4.5hp De Dion	J. Gooding, Elgin Villa, Nacton Road
DX18	2.5hp Ariel	J. Pierce, 20 Silent Street
DX19	8hp De Dion	E. Garnham, 33 Belle Vue Road
DX20	11hp Clement	A. Garnham, 75 Christchurch Street

APPENDIX B

The First Driving Licences Issued by the County Borough of Ipswich,
from January 1904

Licence No	Name	Address
1	J. Pipe	1 Corn Hill
2	E. Sayer	Hurstlea, 7 Warrington Road
3	L. Vulliamy	12 Northgate Street
4	N. Adlard	96 Christchurch Street
5	G. West	123 Lacey Street
6	J. Lewis	52 Myrtle Road
7	J. Pierce	20 Silent Street
8	H. Routh	Westerfield Hall
9	J. Bennett	22 Church Street

10	H. Winkworth	Jupiter Road
11	A. Last	24 Butter Market
12	G. Double	Kirby Lodge, Kirby Street
13	G. Watson	22 Westgate Street
14	J. Egerton	Malpas Cottage, Rushmere
15	A. Newby	9 Warwick Road
16	C. Edwards	25 Lower Brook Street
17	E. Bartlett	153 Norwich Road
18	H. Kettle	24 Lower Brook Street
19	F. Hildyard	79 Princes Street
20	J. Daniels	6 Norwich Road

APPENDIX C

Excerpts from Lamberts Almanacs Relating to Early Motoring Topics

1901 Accident to Mr Scott's (Foxboro Hall, Melton) motor car at Colchester.
      Accident to Rev Flory of Theberton, caused by horse being frightened by a motor car.

1903 Motor Cycle accident to Mr Brown of Ipswich at Warren Hill, Woodbridge.

1905 Motor Cycle stolen from Mr Castell of Wickham Market.
      Car accident at Saxtead.
      General Booth visits Saxmundham, Wickham Market, Woodbridge and Ipswich on his motor car tour.

1906 Messrs Fred Smith and Co's window smashed by Mr G. Stuart Ogilvie's motor car (see also 1912).

1907 Mr Harold Dawson of Kesgrave collided with a motor car and sustained, among other injuries, a fractured nose.
      Horse belonging to Mr Hatcher frightened by motor car and ran away at Framlingham, narrow escape of two men.
      Motor car belonging to Mr Stannard of Eyke destroyed by fire at Campsey Ash.

1908 Motor accident at Helmingham, when Rev Gale Rew of Framsden collided with a horse and trap.
      Serious accident to Mr Maulden, junior, of Framlingham, at Wickham Market Five Cross Ways, by being knocked down by a motor car.

1909 Collision between motor car and horse and trap on Wickham Market Hill.

1910 Young man at Ufford knocked down by motor car and seriously injured.
      Six-year-old killed by motor car in Woodbridge.
      'Poll' (Horace Reynolds), traffic conductor of Woodbridge, dies.

1911 T.E. Riggs of Aldeburgh met with a fatal motorcycle accident at the Cross Corner, Woodbridge.

1912 Collision at Leiston between Stuart Ogilvie's motor car and a horse and cart.

1913 Motor car and motorcycle collision at Marlesford.
      Aeroplane seen flying over Wickham Market!

1914 Motor gymkhana at Rendham Park.
      Motor cars in collision at Cross Corner, Woodbridge, one belonging to Mr A. Adams.

It will be noted that Woodbridge features prominently in the above excerpts. There are two possible reasons for this – the Almanacs were published by Arthur Fairweather of Woodbridge, and there were considerable developments in motoring in that area, perhaps more so than in other small market towns.

By 1909 the Almanacs specifically covered events in Woodbridge, Framlingham, Saxmundham, Leiston, Aldeburgh, Wickham Market and Halesworth and therefore represented a reasonable cross-section of that area.

APPENDIX D

Early Motoring Firms from Kelly's Directory of Suffolk

MA=Motor Agent, MCD=Motor Car Dealer, MCP=Motor Car Proprietor, MCR= Motor Car Repairer, MCA=Motor Car Agent, MCE=Motor Car Engineer, ME=Motor Engineer, MCG=Motor Car Garage, MCM=Motor Car Manufacturer, MAD=Motor Accessory Dealer, MCBB=Motor Car Body Builder.

1900

Anglian Cycle & Engineering Co Ltd, Anglian Works, Stowmarket	MCP
Youngs, W.R., 5 Surrey Street, Lowestoft	MCM

1904

Anglian Motor Co Ltd, Station Road and Newgate Street, Beccles	MCM
Botwood & Egerton, showrooms and garage, Carr Street, and at Woodbridge Road, St Johns, Ipswich	ME, MCM
Brooke & Co, John Walter, Alexandra Road, Lowestoft	ME
Castell, C.D., Wickham Market	ME
Durrants Motors Ltd, Horn Hill, Mill Road, Lowestoft	MCM
Garnham, Alfred, 34 Woodbridge Road, Ipswich	MCD, MCG
Manthorpe, Stanley, 21 High Street, Lowestoft	ME
Parr, Alfred, 183 High Street, Lowestoft	MA
Smith, S. & Co, Bridge Street, Halesworth	MCM
Stannard & Co, Station Road, Stowmarket	MCM
Swan Hotel, Southwold	MCG
Warren & Co, Cullingham Road, Ipswich	ME
Youngs, W.R., 5 Surrey Street, Lowestoft	MCP

1908

Adams, A., Thoroughfare, Woodbridge	MCG
Anglian Motor Co Ltd, Beccles	MCM
Atterton, John, Iron Works, Haverhill	MCG
Bloys, George, 18 Gainsborough Street, Sudbury	MBB
Botwood & Egerton, Ipswich	MCG, ME, MCP, MCM
Brock, W.H. & Co, 67 St Matthews Street, Ipswich	ME
Brock, W.H., St Andrews Street South, Bury St Edmunds	MCM
Brooke, J.W. & Co., Lowestoft	MCM, ME
Burrells, Angel Hill, Bury St Edmunds	ME, MCD MCG
Bury St Edmunds Hotel Co Ltd, The Angel Hotel	MCG
Canham, Frederick, St Matthews Street, Great White Horse Hotel Yard and Portmans Road and Princes Street, Ipswich	ME, MCBB

Castell, C.D., Wickham Market	ME
Claydon, C. & Co, 49 High Street, Haverhill	MCR
Cotton, C., Grundisburgh, Woodbridge	MCG
Day & Page, 20 Foundation Street, Ipswich	ME
Deeks, J. & Sons, Nethergate Street, Clare	MBB
Doe, Charles, Stoke, Clare	MCR
Garnham, Alfred & Co, Woodbridge Road, Ipswich	ME, MCD, MCG
	MCG
Gooding, H. & Son, Market Place, Stowmarket	MCG
Hesworth Co, Haverhill	ME
Hunt, George, Crown and Castle Hotel, Orford	MCG
Ipswich Motor Co, Princes Street, Ipswich	ME
Jeyes, H. & Co, 21 High Street, Lowestoft	ME
Kettle, George, 24 Lower Brook Street, Ipswich	MCG
Matthew, Ernest, Langer Road, Felixstowe	MCG
Mustard & Whitmore, 95 London Road, Ipswich	ME
Orbell Bros, High Street, Clare	MCR
Parr, Alfred, Lowestoft	MA
Pettit, J. & Sons, Crown Street, Mustow Street and Angel Hill,	
Bury St Edmunds	MCM, MCG
Potter, A.G., Station Road, Framlingham	MA
Savory Smith Ltd, 17 Waveney Road, Lowestoft	ME, MCG
Sawyer, S.G., Wrentham, Wangford	ME
Scottorn, F., 19A Portman's Road, Ipswich	ME
Shipp, Albert, Botesdale, Diss	ME
Smith, S. & Co, Halesworth	MCM
Southwold Electric Supply (The Coast Development Co Ltd),	
Electricity Works, St Edmunds Road, Southwold	MCE, MCG
Stannard, Ernest, Eyke, Woodbridge	MA, MCG
Stannard & Co (Agents), Stowmarket	MCM
Swan Hotel, Southwold	MCGE
Warren & Co, 139 London Road, Ipswich	MCG
Warren, W. & Co, Cullingham Road, Ipswich	ME
Wiffen, Chas, Church Street, Clare	MA
Zissell, George, White Hart Hotel, Wickham Market	MCG

1912

Adams, A., Thoroughfare, Woodbridge	MCG
Bloys, George, 18 Gainsborough Street, Sudbury	MCBB
Botwoods Ltd, showrooms and garage, Carr Street, and	MCM,
484, 486 Woodbridge Road, Ipswich	MCG, ME
	MCBB,
	MCP
Burrell's, Angel Hill, Bury St Edmunds	MCD
Bury St Edmunds Hotel Co Ltd, The Angel Hotel, Bury St Edmunds	MCG
Canham, Frederick, St Matthews Street, Portmans Road and Princess	
Street, Ipswich	ME, MCBB
Castell, Charles, Wickham Market	ME, MCA
Charlish, Robert, Earsham St, Bungay	MCG
Deeks, J. & Sons, Nethergate Street, Clare	MCBB

Digby, Scolney, Cornhill, Bury St Edmunds	MCG
Eastern Counties Garage, Crown Street, Ipswich	ME
Egertons, 3 and 5 Northgate Street, Ipswich	ME, MAD, MCG
Fairweather, Walter, Wellclose Square, Framlingham	MCP
Foreman & Donaghy, 47 Thoroughfare, Halesworth	ME
Fulcher, Lionel, private landaulettes and touring cars for hire, 10 Whiting Street, Bury St Edmunds	MCG, MA, MCP
Garnham, Arthur, Cumberland Street, Woodbridge	MCG
Garnham, A.F. & Co, Ipswich	ME
Garrard, Charles, Market Hill, Framlingham	MCA, MCE, MCG
Goldsmith, D. 16 Clarkson Street, Ipswich	ME
Gooding, H. & Son, Market Place, Stowmarket	MCG
Hanbury & Co, High Street, Brandon	MCA
Harrison, John, Tavern Street, Ipswich	MCG
Hesworth Co, Haverhill	ME
Hitchcock, Walter, Station, Elmswell, Bury St Edmunds	ME
Hughes & Hammond, Fornham Road, Bury St Edmunds	MCE
Hunt, G., Crown and Castle Hotel, Orford	MCG
James, Talbot & Davison Ltd, Horn Hill, Lowestoft	ME
Jenkins, James, Bury St Edmunds	MCM, MCR, MCP, ME, MCD, MCG, MA
Kettle, George & Co, 24 Lower Brook Street, Ipswich	MCG
Lowestoft Motor Co Ltd, 97 & 99 London Road South, Lowestoft	MCE
Miller, F. & Co, Oulton Broad, Lowestoft	ME
Moss, H.G., 345 Woodbridge Road, Ipswich	MCR
Nice, T.H. & Co, 21 Abbeygate Street, Bury St Edmunds	MCE
Page & Girling, Melton, Woodbridge	ME
Parr, Alfred, Lowestoft	MA
Pettitt, James, St Andrews Street South, Bury St Edmunds	MCE, MCG
Pettitt, J. & Sons, Mustow Street and Crown Street, Bury St Edmunds	MCG, MCR, MCM
Potter, A.G., Framlingham	MA
Pratt, R.W., Hamilton Road, Felixstowe	MCG
Robinson, William, Anglian Motor Works, Newgate and Station Road, Beccles	MCM
Sawyer, S.G., Wrentham, Wangford	ME
Smith, Clarence, High Street, Clare	MCR
Smith, G.D. & Son, 43 Anglesea Road, Ipswich	MCP
Smith & Wesby, Saxmundham	ME
Southwold Electric Supply (The Coast Development Corporation Ltd) Electricity Works, St Edmunds Road, Southwold	MCE, MCG
Stannard & Co (agents), Stowmarket	MCM
Stannard, Ernest, Eyke	MA, MCG
St Georges Motor & Engineering Co Ltd, St Georges Street, Ipswich	ME, MCG
Stowe, William, 25 Commercial Road, Lowestoft	ME
Swan Hotel, Southwold	MCG
Toombs, C., North Terrace Road, Mildenhall	MCA
Ward & Son, High Street, Aldeburgh	MCG

1912 – Entries per Town

Ipswich	11
Bury St Edmunds	10
Lowestoft	5
Framlingham	3
Woodbridge	3
Clare	2
Southwold	2
Stowmarket	2

Note: only towns with more than one entry are listed here.

The number of categories for inclusion in the Directory seems rather excessive, and probably does not truly reflect a company's overall business interests. Alfred Adams of Woodbridge, for example, is only listed as having a motor car garage, whereas it is known that he had been selling and repairing cars and motorcycles for several years. There would also have been several firms who were not included in the directory for various reasons.

APPENDIX E

Early Registration Marks For Suffolk

		Introduced
East Suffolk	BJ	December 1903
	ABJ	October 1933
	BBJ	April 1935
	CBJ	September 1936
	DBJ	1938
	EBJ	July 1939
	RT	May 1925
	ART	July 1934
	BRT	January 1936
	CRT	April 1937
	DRT	October 1938
West Suffolk	CF	1904
	GV	July 1930
	ACF	April 1946
County Borough of Ipswich	DX	1904
	PV	July 1932
	ADX	January 1950

For all the two-letter marks, the numbers followed to 9999. Once the three-letter system was introduced, it only allowed numbers to 999, which soon exhausted the alphabet. At this point, the numbers were placed in front of the letters, which extended the life again. In 1964, the 'year' letter B was introduced in Suffolk, to fall in line with the need to use seven-digit registration. Only East Suffolk had come close to using up the old system, as Ipswich and West Suffolk had not even started on the reversed numbers.

BIBLIOGRAPHY

There are a great number of books available on specific areas of motoring and individual makes, but the following provide useful background reading.

Adeney, M., *The Motor Makers – The Turbulent History of Britain's Car Industry*, Collins, 1988

Allen, M., *Anglia Prefect Popular,* Motor Racing Publications, 1986

Bacon, R., *British Motorcycles of the 1930s*, Osprey Publishing Ltd

Burgess Wise, D., *Veteran and Vintage Cars,* The Hamlyn Publishing Group Ltd, 1970

Cooke, S., *This Motoring,* Automobile Association

Edge S.F., *My Motoring Reminisences,* G.T. Foulis & Co Ltd

Edwards, H., *The Morris Motor Car 1913–1983,* Moorland Publishing Co Ltd., 1983

The First 75 years, Automobile Association

Flower, R., and M. Wynn Jones, *One Hundred Years of Motoring*, The Royal Automobile Club, 1981

Georgano, G.N. (ed), *The Complete Encyclopedia of Motor Cars, 1885 to the Present*, Ebury Press (3rd edition)

Golden Milestone - 50 Years of the AA, Automobile Association, 1955

Harding, A. (ed), *The Guinness Book of Car Facts and Feats*, Guinness Superlatives Ltd

Herridge, C., *Motorcycles of the 20s and 30s*, Temple Press, 1985

Ixion, *Motor Cycle Cavalcade,* Iliffe & Sons Ltd, 1950

Johnson, E., *The Dawn of Motoring,* Mercedes Benz (UK) Ltd, 1986

Lacey, R., *Ford,* William Heinemann Ltd.

Lane, A., *Motoring Costume,* Shire Publications Ltd (197)

Lord Montague of Beaulieu and F. Wilson McComb, *Behind the Wheel, The Magic and Manners of Early Motoring*, Paddington Press Ltd

Morley, D., *The Story of the Motorcycle,* Dean's International Publishing, 1983

Morris, L.E., *The Country Garage,* Shire Publications Ltd (129)

Nicholson, T.R., *Sprint,* David & Charles, 1969

— *The Birth of the British Motor Car,* Volumes 1, 2, 3, The MacMillan Press Ltd, 1982

Plowden, W., *The Motor Car And Politics, 1896–1970*, The Bodley Head

Scott-Moncrieff, D., *Veteran and Edwardian Motor Cars*, B.T. Batsford Ltd, 1961

Sedgwick, M., *Cars of the Thirties & Forties*, The Hamlyn Publishing Group Ltd

Sorensen, L., *The Ford Road,* Silverdale Publishing Co

Thacker, T., *32 Ford, The Deuce,* Osprey Publishing Ltd, 1984

Tragatsch, E., *The Illustrated Encyclopedia of Motorcycles*, The Hamlyn Publishing Group Ltd, 1977

Turner, D., *Ford Popular and Other Side Valves*, Osprey Publishing Ltd

INDEX

(Illustrations in bold type)